LAKE SUPERIOR'S "SHIPWRECK COAST"

A Survey of Maritime Accidents from Whitefish Bay's Point Iroquois to Grand Marais, Michigan.

By
FREDERICK STONEHOUSE

Cover Illustration

The cover illustration shows the wreck of the steamer H.E. RUNNELS lost off Grand Marais in November 14, 1919. The illustration is the work of Edward Pusick of Wyoming, Michigan. Known as the "Master of Disaster" for his preference of only illustrating vessels in the act of sinking, he is one of the finest of the Great Lakes maritime artists.

LAKE SUPERIOR'S "SHIPWRECK COAST"

A Survey of Maritime Accidents from Whitefish Bay's Point Iroquois to Grand Marais, Michigan

Copyright 1985

ISBN 0-932212-43-3
Library of Congress No. 85-70794

By Frederick Stonehouse & Avery Color Studios
Marquette, Michigan   Au Train, Michigan

Published by
Avery Color Studios
Au Train, Michigan 49806

First Edition - March 1985

CONTENTS

Author's Note

This book is not intended to be the "end all" to the story of the shipwrecks of the Whitefish area. Rather, it is only a survey.

Some incidents are treated in greater depth and detail than others. My determination was essentially subjective if I felt the incident illustrated a specific problem, either in terms of the wreck itself, or subsequent involvement of the U.S. Life-Saving Service/ Coast Guard, I provided greater detail.

Should the reader desire to learn more of the incident, or question the data, bibliographic information follows each wreck. To take the time to complete a book such as this and not provide such references is, in my opinion, cheating the reader. There certainly are other references available for each wreck. I did not list them all. Those cited are the ones from which the material was drawn.

I would like to say the book is 100% complete in terms of all wrecks having been included. However, experience tells me there certainly are omissions. In compiling a survey like this, the researcher works from a hodge-podge of sources. There is no master list of wrecks from which to simply pull the information from. You have to dig, sift, worm and extricate data from literally hundreds of documents. You hope you are complete, but you know that without fail something may have slipped through.

Some judgment was used concerning which wrecks were included and which ones were omitted. My rational was thus; if it went ashore between Waiska Bay and Grand Marais, I included it. An earlier book, MUNSING SHIPWRECKS, included those wrecks between Au Sable Point, just to the west of Grand Marais and Au Train Point 35 miles farther west.

8

The offshore wrecks presented the biggest problem. Generally, if the wreck's location was most often taken from the survey coast limits, as in "25 miles northwest of Whitefish Point", I included it. It is quite possible there are some omissions as a result of this methodology. For those wrecks in which the location of loss was not known, I simply used my best guess. Regrettably there is no way of using a clear, indisputable line of geographic demarcation separating those wrecks in and out of the survey limits.

It is interesting to speculate on the value of feeding all known wreck data into a computer and using it to plot the locations. However, given the often conflicting reports on loss locations, it would only be a case of "garbage in, garbage out". But perhaps someday..........

This is not a diver's guide. The directions and locations are not intended to be accurate enough to find the wrecks.

I used additional subjective judgment as to whether a wreck was included in the main text or in the "additional" section. Generally the major incidents were kept in the main text and minor ones in the additional. However there were some exceptions, especially when the particular circumstance of an accident was interesting or when the incident high-lighted a special danger of the area. The additional list is not complete, but does well illustrate the large number of vessel accidents and reoccurring problems.

I would certainly appreciate any help from readers concerning omissions, errors or suggestions.

ACKNOWLEDGEMENTS

Producing a study of this nature by necessity requires a tremendous amount of assistance from a number of people and institutions. It was only through their willing and professional help this study was produced. I would like to thank the following:

Tom Farnquist and the Great Lakes Shipwreck Historical Society

Jean Olson

C. Patrick Labadie and the Lake Superior Marine Museum

Marine Collection, Milwaukee Public Library

Marquette County Historical Society

Marquette Maritime Museum

National Archives and Records Service

Peter White Public Library

Ken E. Thro

Venture North and Tom Bathey

INTRODUCTION

If there is truly a graveyard of Lake Superior, it is the general area of Whitefish Point. More vessels have been lost there than any other part of the lake. There are essentially three reasons for this terrible toll.

First, the eastern end of the lake is a very congested area. Whitefish Bay acts like a huge funnel, gathering in the downbound vessel traffic from Duluth, Marquette, Thunder Bay, Two Harbors and all of the other ports, squeezing it together and directing it down to the St. Mary's River and the Soo Canal. By itself this presents no great problem, except that all of the upbound traffic must pass through all the downbound traffic. Since nearly the beginning of navigation a system of separate upbound and downbound shipping lanes helped to keep matters fairly straight. I say fairly because there are numerous examples of collisions between upbound and downbound vessels occurring in perfect conditions, designated lanes not withstanding. A case in point is the tragic August 20, 1920 loss of the SUPERIOR CITY.

The truly terrible consequences of the Whitefish Bay funnel happened when visibility decreased, which is reason number two. In some cases smoke from forest fires was the culprit, in others it was snow squalls. But by far the worst problem was the legendary Lake Superior fogs. In some cases sailors claimed the cold grey curtain had to be cut with a knife. The fog caused vessels not only to collide, but also to run aground. Either could have dire consequences. Before radar, fog, smoke or snow were deadly.

The third reason for the carnage of wrecks was the great sweep of the seas. A Lake Superior storm usually screams down from the northwest and can

11

build a sea of monstrous proportions. A roaring northwester can build waves over a clear sweep of 160 miles of open water. When the 729-foot EDMUND FITZGERALD sank 17 miles northwest of Whitefish Point on November 10, 1975, the seas offshore were reported at a height of 30 feet plus! The nightmarish effect of waves of this size on the vessels of a century ago can only be imagined.

Even comparatively light storms caused problems, as evidenced by the many vessels, both sail and steam, blown ashore by the north winds. Always it was the wind, the cold north wind that spelled trouble. In fact it was as a result of this Storm God from the north that the stretch of coast from Whitefish Point west to Grand Marais was called the "shipwreck coast."

Superior is the greatest of the Great Lakes. She's the largest in both surface area and volume, the deepest, the clearest, the coldest and, in this age of pollution, the cleanest. By any standard, Superior is the queen of the Great Lakes.

But just as she portrays a special majesty in her "positive" attributes, she also displays a devastating malevolence in her fury.

When, as songwriter Gordon Lightfoot put it, "the waves turn the minutes into hours," the lake is truly awesome. Stated a little differently, the lady can also be a tramp.

Since navigation began, Lake Superior has exacted its toll of shipwrecks. To date, approximately 550 have been recorded. The reasons aren't unusual, storm, fire and collision are the most common. Their locations as could be expected tend to be around those areas of greatest hazard, shoals and reefs, congested shipping lanes and particularly rough stretches of water.

As this book illustrates, the toll of wrecks has noticeably decreased in recent times. The reasons are many. The vessels have become bigger and generally safer. They are now equipped with radar to help prevent thick weather problems and LORAN to aid in positively fixing vessel locations. Modern radio allows the vessels to keep in contact with other vessels as well as the shore. Weather forecasting has greatly improved and rare is the unexpected blow. Regular weather broadcasts keep vessels aware of any expected change. Improved aids to navigation, buoys, lights and radio beacons also play a role, as does periodic Coast Guard radio broadcasts advising mariners of changes or problems.

There also are fewer wrecks because there are less vessels. In 1880 there were 3,127 commercial vessels navigating the lakes. Today, there are perhaps only 200!

But regardless of the number of vessels, the Whitefish area remains one of the most dangerous on the Great Lakes. It well deserves the title of "The Graveyard of Lake Superior."

Marquette Harbor circa 1865. As the original iron port on Lake Superior, much of the vessel traffic along the shipwreck coast was either upbound to, or downbound from Marquette.

Marquette County Historical Society

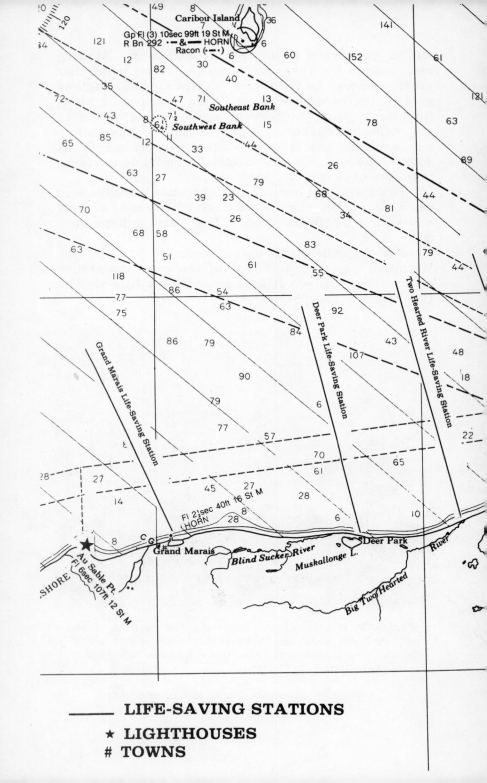

LIFE-SAVING STATIONS

★ **LIGHTHOUSES**

\# **TOWNS**

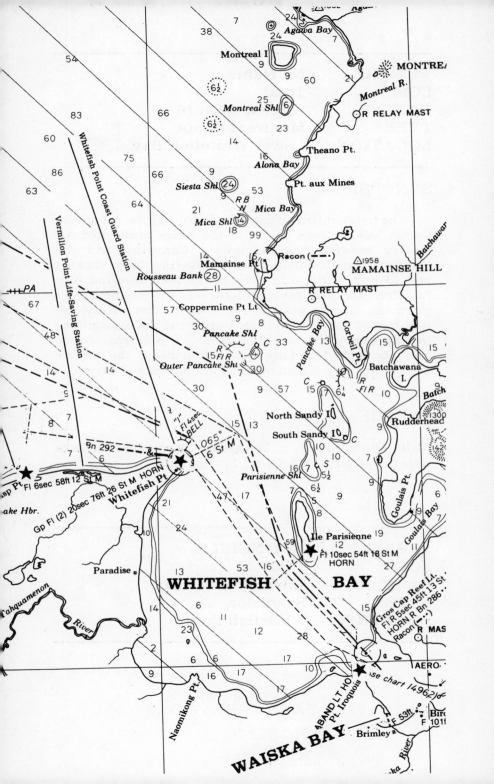

VESSEL:	No Name
LOSS:	Total
DATE:	August 26, 1816
TYPE:	Montreal Canoe
LOCATION:	Lower Whitefish Bay

SYNOPSIS:

The first confirmed casualty involving a commercial vessel was a direct result of the fierce, unbridled fur rivalry between the Northwest Company and the Hudson's Bay Company. After capturing the Northwest post at Fort William in the western lake, the Hudson's Bay Company sent several Montreal canoes of prisoners down the lake to eastern Canada. In lower Whitefish Bay one of the sail equipped craft capsized, resulting in approximately ten fatalities. A Montreal canoe was about 36 feet long, six feet wide at the middle and could carry a load of three to four tons of cargo.

REFERENCES:

Wolff, Dr. Julius F. Jr., "Canadian Shipwrecks on Lake Superior." INLAND SEAS, Spring 1978.

VESSEL:	INVINCIBLE
LOSS:	Total
DATE:	November 14, 1816
TYPE:	Schooner
LOCATION:	Whitefish Point

SNYOPSIS:

Enroute from Fort William to the Soo, this small schooner was overtaken by a north gale, driving her ashore in the vicinity of Whitefish Point. The schooner was destroyed but those aboard were uninjured.

REFERENCES

"Narrative of Jean Baptiste Perraut," MICHIGAN PIONEER AND HISTORICAL COLLECTIONS, Volume 37, 1909 - 1910.

VESSEL:	**MANHATTAN**
LOSS:	**Recovered**
DATE:	**August 4, 1851**
TYPE:	**Wooden Propeller**
LOCATION:	**Parisienne Island**

SYNOPSIS:

In 1851 there were only four steamboats on all of Lake Superior, but incredibly two of them collided! Apparently while trying to pass close aboard each other near Parisienne Island, the two vessels, the propellers MANHATTAN and MONTICELLO, confused signals and the MONTICELLO rammed the MANHATTAN on her starboard quarter. Within five minutes the MANHATTAN settled in shallow water up to her upper works. The MONTICELLO was apparently not damaged but did founder a month later west of the Keweenaw. It was never clearly determined if she had suffered unknown damage in the MANHATTAN collision or sank as a result of damage from striking an underwater obstacle shortly before her loss.

With the MONTICELLO assisting, the MANHATTAN was later raised and repaired. The 319-ton MANHATTAN was new on the lake, having just been portaged over the Soo the year before. She was built in Cleveland in 1847.

An interesting observation to the accident was provided by the Reverend John H. Pitezel, one of the early Methodist missionaries. Relating the incident in his book LIGHTS AND SHADES OF MISSIONARY LIFE, he wrote, "...the passengers on the MONTICELLO had just been dancing, a thing of common occurrence on the Lake Superior boats, and at the time of the collision, were partaking of an oyster supper. Thus are people often in the hight (sic) of conviviality, intoxicated by trifling amusement and sinful diversion; as thoughtless about their souls as though they had none, and indifferent about the retributions of eternity as if such things were ideal dreams, when "there is but a step between them and death".

REFERENCES:

LAKE SUPERIOR JOURNAL. August 13, December 1, 1851.

Pitezel, Rev. John H. LIGHTS AND SHADES OF MISSIONARY LIFE. (New York: Walden and Stowe, 1883).

VESSEL:	**B.L. WEBB**
LOSS:	**Recovered**
DATE:	**November 1856**
TYPE:	**Wooden Propeller**
LOCATION:	**Waiska Bay, Whitefish Bay**

SYNOPSIS:

After stranding in Waiska Bay, about five miles southwest of Point Iroquois, the 195-foot, 843-ton, B.L. WEBB burned with the loss of one life. Built in Detroit in 1856 by J. and S. Jenkins, she was owned by the Detroit and Lake Superior Company.

In 1856 the hull was salvaged and rebuilt as the propeller MARQUETTE. She sailed as a steamer until 1870 when her engines were lifted and she was converted to a schooner. In 1888, she was out of service.

REFERENCES:

LAKE SUPERIOR JOURNAL. November 27, 1856.
Lake Superior Marine Museum Archives. Duluth, Minnesota.
Lytle, William M. and Holdcamper, Forrest R., Comp. MERCHANT VESSELS OF THE UNITED STATES, 1790 - 1868. (Staten Island, New York: The Steamboat Historical Society of America, 1975).
Mansfield, J.B., comp. HISTORY OF THE GREAT LAKES. (Chicago: J.H. Beers and Co. 1899).

VESSEL:	**INDIANA**
LOSS:	**Total**
DATE:	**June 6, 1858**
TYPE:	**Propeller**
LOCATION:	**Off Crisp Point**

SYNOPSIS:

On June 6, 1858 the 350-ton propeller INDIANA was five miles north-northeast of Crisp Point and proceeding without trouble through stormy seas. She had just left Marquette and was carrying a heavy load of 280 tons of iron ore as well as some general package freight.

Without warning the INDIANA started to fill with water, apparently from a ruptured seal on her propeller shaft. When the crew tried to reach the seal through the crawlway, they found it blocked by an extra ton of ore. It was thought the damage to the seal was done when the INDIANA cracked her sternpost in the heavy seas.

The pumps were unable to keep up with the leak, so within 15 minutes the 21 people aboard, including her owner, Frank Perew, abandoned her in the yawl. She stayed afloat for quite awhile, sinking in two hours on an even keel. The survivors reached shore safely. The INDIANA was a $12,000 loss.

Originally the INDIANA ran in general passenger and freight trade in Lakes Erie, Huron and Michigan, serving the small ports along the shore. When the Soo Canal opened in 1855, she began runs to Lake Superior, carrying passengers and freight up and iron ore, copper and freight down. The ore was usually carried on the decks and the more valuable package freight below.

The INDIANA had a history of trouble. In April 1851 she had a minor collision with the schooner CAMBRIA; in April 1854 she struck a pier in Cleveland harbor "...doing considerable damage"; October 1854 saw her on the rocks in the St. Mary's River; September 1856 she was ashore at Point Abino; and in Ocotober 1857 she again struck the Cleveland pier. Navigation in the early days of Great Lakes commerce was tough and demanding; there were few lights and marked channels so the long list of INDIANA problems was not that unusual.

The INDIANA was built in 1848 at Vermilion, Ohio by Joseph M. Keating. Double decked, she had a listed capacity of 500 tons. Carrying a single mast forward, the propeller was 146.4-feet in length and 23-feet in beam. In general construction, the INDIANA was very similar to the more popular sidewheeler hulls in that she had large sponsons overhanging her hull to increase capacity.

The INDIANA was one of a new class of vessels known as "propellers" because they used the novel "Erickson screw propeller." The new class revolutionized the freight trade. They provided greater capacity and were more economical than the sidewheelers. Their smaller engines pushed rather than pulled the vessel through the water as did the old sidewheeler's paddles. Since the engines were placed further aft, more room was available for freight and passengers. In the late 1840s, through the 1850s, and 1860s, the new propellers proved more and more popular.

The U.S. Army Corps of Engineers barge COLEMAN. The INDIANA's boiler is visible on deck.

Lake Superior Marine Museum

The INDIANA was quickly forgotten until 1972

when the famous Great Lakes diver John Steele discovered her. He found her in 118-feet of water on an even keel on a sandy bottom. Most important, she was largely intact. Eagerly he filmed the wreck, carefully documenting her condition.

When the film was distributed to marine historians, great excitement was generated. The old INDIANA was considered to be one of the most important shipwreck discoveries on the Great Lakes.

The reason for the excitement was the INDIANA's remarkably primitive machinery, 40 years older than that of any other surviving Great Lakes vessel. The film showed it all in amazing detail. It was evident the machinery predated by 30 years even any technical drawings or plans of similar devices! The film for the first time provided a record of an actual example of an 1840's era screw propeller, a vessel often mentioned in historical documents but never before available for "touch."

The engine was considered the simplest form of a vertical reciprocating steam engine coupled to one of the earliest Erickson propellers. It stood nearly 18-feet high, including the large oak frame. The machinery was in a near perfect state of preservation and could provide an immense amount of historical information.

In 1979, through the cooperation of the State of Michigan, National Trust for Historical Preservation, National Council on Historic Preservation, U.S. Navy, Army Corps of Engineers, U.S. Coast Guard and Smithsonian Institution, the machinery of the INDIANA was raised for restoration and display in the Smithsonian's National Museum of History and Technology.

The actual salvage work was done by a Navy dive team working from the Corps of Engineers derrick barge COLEMAN, tender BAYFIELD and tug LAKE SUPERIOR. The operation lasted 12 days and resulted in the recovery of the 18-foot tall engine, 13-foot high boiler, 10-foot diameter Erickson propeller, steam condenser, hot water feed, steering quadrant, throttle and fire box. Despite 121 years under water, the engine's wood and metal were excellently preserved because of the fresh water and cold temperatures.

The importance of the INDIANA can't be over emphasized. The Smithsonian stated the "engine of the INDIANA represents the earliest marine steam plant still in existence in North America which had an actual working history."

REFERENCES:

DETROIT FREE PRESS. December 2, 1979.
MARQUETTE MINING JOURNAL. August 6, 8, 21, 23, 1979.
Runge Collection. Milwaukee Public Library.
Wells, H., ed. "History of Accidents, Casualties and Wrecks on Lake Superior" (manuscript compiled for the U.S. Army Corps of Engineers, Duluth, Minnesota, 1938).
Wolff, Dr. Julius F. Jr. "Salvaging the Engines of the INDIANA." INLAND SEAS, Winter 1973.
Wright, Dr. Richard J. "The INDIANA Salvage." DETROIT MARINE HISTORIAN, December 1979.

VESSEL:	**MANHATTAN**
LOSS:	**Total**
DATE:	**September 1, 1859**
TYPE:	**Wooden Propeller**
LOCATION:	**Grand Marais**

SYNOPSIS:

Apparently as the result of a north gale, the 319-ton MANHATTAN, the same vessel that had earlier been rammed and sunk by the MONTICELLO, was driven ashore east of Grand Marais. Owned by Marquette interests, the vessel was a total loss of $7,500. Later her engines, anchors, chains, cables, rigging, furniture and other items were salvaged.

Known as a crack boat, the loss of the MANHATTAN was much lamented by the local paper, which was moved to comment ".......brave old MANHATTAN, thou who hast roughed it through many a storm.......who has oft risen in triumph.......dark o'er the wave....... must yield to inexorable history at last! Long will thy memory be cherished by the many thou hast borne in safety, in sunshine and in storm, along these shores."

Bishop Baraga, the famous "snowshoe priest," was a frequent passenger on the MANHATTAN. It is said that the captain, John McKay, often provided the good priest with his own cabin.

REFERENCES:

LAKE SUPERIOR JOURNAL. September 21, 1859.

VESSEL:	**GREY EAGLE**
LOSS:	**Total**
DATE:	**July 17, 1869**
TYPE:	**Schooner**
LOCATION:	**Whitefish Point**

SYNOPSIS:

The 167-foot, 287-ton GREY EAGLE was destroyed after going aground at Whitefish Point. She was upbound from Chicago for Marquette when lost. She is also listed as the GRAY EAGLE.

REFERENCES:

Mansfield, op. cit.

Wolff, Dr. Julius F. Jr. *THE SHIPWRECKS OF LAKE SUPERIOR. (Duluth, Minnesota: Lake Superior Marine Museum Association, 1979).*

VESSEL:	**W.W. ARNOLD**
LOSS:	**Total**
DATE:	**November 4, 1869**
TYPE:	**Schooner**
LOCATION:	**Big Two Hearted River**

SYNOPSIS:

One of the true schooner, as opposed to schooner-barge, wrecks that occurred in the area was that of the two masted, 426-ton W.W. ARNOLD. The ARNOLD departed Marquette bound for Cleveland with 550 tons of ore at 4 p.m., November 4, 1869. She was under the command of Captain Beardsley and carried two passengers and a crew of eight or nine.

About four hours after she left, a "great gale of wind"accompanied by a blinding snow storm roared down from the northwest. The storm raged for 24 hours and produced some extremely high seas. Mr. Ashman, the lightkeeper at Whitefish Point, said it was the most terrific storm he had ever seen.

Even though the ARNOLD was not reported to have reached the Soo, little concern was initially felt for her. It was thought she was too strong and her captain too experienced to have any serious problems. But as the days passed sailors knew something serious had indeed happened.

On December 7, the worst fears confirmed. An Indian mail carrier arrived in Munising with the news that he had found a wreck on the beach at the mouth of the Big Two Hearted River. An Indian trapper related to the mail carrier that he had counted ten bodies along the water's edge.

The next day four Munising men departed for the wreck, finally arriving four days later after partially rowing, snowshoeing and hiking. The group had travelled 65 long, hard miles.

Four miles from the actual wreck site they started to find pieces of the ARNOLD. The men expected to find the schooner reasonably intact but instead discovered that she was "literally torn to atoms." A piece of her bottom was a third of a mile above the river and part of her forward bulwarks on the lower side. Some evidence of the power of the storm was found on the 40-foot high sand bluffs opposite the wreck site. The cliff tops were littered with pieces of the ARNOLD, including the roof of the pilothouse, boxes, chains, bedding and a smashed yawl. The searchers found no bodies.

The following April another search party discovered the body of the captain and one sailor. Both were buried on the high sand bluffs, opposite the point where the schooner died. Some of the rigging and hardware was later salvaged.

What actually caused the loss was never determined. When one of the search parties discovered that her foremast had broken feet above the deck and that the jaws of the boom showed evidence of having been chopped with an axe, the blame was laid against the broken mast. Without it, the ARNOLD would have been helpless in the tremendous storm. Driven before the towering seas, she probably struck the offshore sandbar, going to pieces very rapidly. None of her crew had a chance of reaching shore alive.

By no means had the ARNOLD been overloaded. On her final trip she loaded only 550 tons of ore. Often she carried 650 tons. The ARNOLD was nearly new, having been built in Buffalo in 1863. Rated A-1 by Lloyds, she was a loss of $19,000.

REFERENCES:

Hall, Captain J.W. *MARINE DISASTERS ON THE WESTERN LAKES DURING THE NAVIGATION SEASON OF 1869. (Detroit: W.E. Tunis, 1870).*
MARQUETTE MINING JOURNAL. November 20, 27, December 18, 25, 1869, January 1, 8, April 9, 25, May 14, 1870.

VESSEL:	**PLOVER**
LOSS:	**Total**
DATE:	**October 12, 1871**
TYPE:	**Schooner**
LOCATION:	**Whitefish Point**

SYNOPSIS:

A fierce north gale stranded and destroyed this 390-ton schooner near Whitefish Point on October 12, 1871. All eight hands reached safety in the yawl. The PLOVER had been downbound from Duluth with a grain cargo when disaster overtook her. She had been built at Milan, Ohio by Merry and Gay in 1857. Owned by Winslow of Cleveland, she was a loss of $28,000.

REFERENCES:

Lake Superior Marine Museum Archives. Duluth, Minnesota.
National Archives. "Microfilm T-729, Marine Casualties

on the Great Lakes. 1863 - 1873,"Record Group 26. Wells, op. cit.

VESSEL:	**SATURN, JUPITER**
LOSS:	**Total**
DATE:	**November 27, 1872**
TYPE:	**Schooner-Barges**
LOCATION:	**Whitefish Point, Vermilion Point**

SYNOPSIS:

Early on the morning of November 27, 1872 the sidewheeler JOHN A. DIX departed Marquette towing the 400-ton schooner-barges JUPITER and SATURN. Both schooner-barges were loaded with iron ore.

Throughout the day the weather worsened. At 5 p.m. off Vermilion Point, the small fleet was struck by a strong north gale. Soon all three vessels were laboring in the rolling seas. Within half an hour, the tow line to the JUPITER parted. An hour later the SATURN broke her cable too. In the dark night and blowing spray, the DIX soon lost sight of the drifting schooner-barges and ran for shelter behind Whitefish Point. That night the temperatures fell to near zero. Doubtlessly the crews suffered terribly. The next morning the DIX reported she had nearly a foot of ice on her decks.

The SATURN was blown aground three miles west of Whitefish Point and the JUPITER 12 miles further west, near the Big Two Hearted River. All of those aboard, 14 men and one woman cook, perished.

Initial reports said both vessels were completely visible, but later ones stated only the masts showed. This apparent discrepancy can be resolved by the scenario of having the vessels first ground on an offshore sandbar and later being swept into deeper water between the bar and shore.

The JUPITER was a loss of $12,000 and the SATURN $13,000. Both were owned by E.B. Ward.

REFERENCES:

CHICAGO TRIBUNE. January 30, 1873.
MARQUETTE MINING JOURNAL. December 7, 21, 1872.
Wells, op. cit.

VESSEL:	**W.C. GRISWOLD**
LOSS:	**Total**
DATE:	**November 27, 1872**
TYPE:	**Schooner**
LOCATION:	**Gros Cap, Whitefish Bay**

SYNOPSIS:

The same fierce storm that sank the JUPITER and SATURN also destroyed the 354-ton, three masted schooner W.C. GRISWOLD. The GRISWOLD was downbound with grain when she disappeared with all hands. It is thought she came to grief near Gros Cap since schooner masts were sighted there. She was a loss of $27,000. Owned by W. Lane of Sandusky, Ohio, she was built in 1854 at Vermilion, Ohio by M.A. Bradley. In some sources she is also listed as the CHARLES G. GRISWOLD.

REFERENCES:

Lake Superior Marine Museum Archives. Duluth, Minnesota.
Wells, op. cit.
Wolff, SHIPWRECKS OF LAKE SUPERIOR, op. cit.
Wolff, Dr. Julius F. Jr. "They Sailed Away on Lake Superior." INLAND SEAS, Winter 1973.

VESSEL:	**W.O. BROWN**
LOSS:	**Total**
DATE:	**November 27, 1872**
TYPE:	**Schooner**
LOCATION:	**Point Mamainse, Ontario**

SYNOPSIS:

The 400-ton two masted schooner W.O. BROWN became the fourth vessel sunk by the November 27-28, 1872 storm. The BROWN had departed Duluth on November 23, bound for Buffalo with wheat. On November 27, in the vicinity of Whitefish Point, she was overtaken by the screaming gale. Some reports suggest the winds blew from the southwest first and later switched to the northwest, a typical event for a powerful Superior hell-bender.

Initially the BROWN was reported lost with all hands. Later events proved this conclusion false.

The storm drove the BROWN into shallow water in a small cove near Point Mamainse where the huge breakers literally tore her apart. She was so far ashore that when the mainmast fell, it touched the beach. As the waves worked over the BROWN, six crewmen were swept to their deaths. Only three of the crew reached shore alive.

To survive the intense cold, the men built a fire in the schooner's cabin, which had been battered loose from the BROWN and swept ashore. For food they boiled the raw wheat from her cargo into a kind of gruel. Salvaging what they could from the wreck they set about the very serious task of surviving.

When the weather finally moderated the sailors built a raft and used it to recover the yawl, miraculously still partially intact and wedged on some offshore rocks. The repairs to the yawl and preparation took ten days, but finally on December 7, they coasted along the shore south to Batchawana Bay. There they located a lumber camp and shelter. Eventually the sailors recovered and reached their homes. The BROWN was a loss of $24,000.

REFERENCES

GREAT LAKES SHIPWRECK QUARTERLY. Volume 1, Number 4.
MARQUETTE MINING JOURNAL. December 7, 21, 1872.
Wells, op. cit.

VESSEL:	ATHENIAN
LOSS:	Recovered
DATE:	1873
TYPE:	Schooner
LOCATION:	Waiska Bay, Whitefish Bay

SYNOPSIS:

THE 372-ton schooner ATHENIAN stranded in Waiska Bay as a result of a rolling north gale. In the spring of 1874 she was pulled free and taken to Detroit for repairs. This same type of accident, the storm stranding of a schooner, was one to be repeated again and again. She was built in 1856 at Buffalo by J.C. Jones. The ATHENIAN ended her days as a shipwreck near Oscoda in 1880.

REFERENCES:

Lake Superior Marine Museum Archives. Duluth, Minnesota.
National Archives, T-279, op. cit.
MARQUETTE MINING JOURNAL. June 13, 1874.

VESSEL:	**COMET**
LOSS:	**Total**
DATE:	**August 26, 1875**
TYPE:	**Wooden Propeller**
LOCATION:	**Whitefish Bay**

SYNOPSIS:

The 181-foot, 621-ton wooden propeller COMET was a victim of a Whitefish Bay collision. At about 8 p.m., August 26, she rounded Whitefish Point downbound for Buffalo with a mixed cargo of silver ore, copper ore and pig iron. Her course was roughly southeast, at least until she made Point Iroquois Light when she would swing into the Soo. She had departed Duluth on the 23rd, but had stopped briefly at several south shore posts. Her last stop was at Munising.

Through the dusk, the lookouts spotted a white light ahead, then a red one. The COMET's master, Francis Dugot, swung his vessel to port, reportedly gave a blast on his whistle and slowed. Suddenly a green light was sighted. Captain Dugot had brought the COMET across the bows of another vessel!

Although Captain Dugot tried to swing the COMET clear of the onrushing vessel, he was too late. With a crash the sidewheeler MANITOBA, cut deeply into the COMET about 20 feet forward of the stern. Fatally damaged, the COMET sank stern first in ten minutes. Eleven men went down with her. The MANITOBA stopped and rescued ten survivors, including the captain.

The wooden propeller COMET, lost in a collision with the MANITOBA on August 25, 1875.

To truly understand the detail and horror of the event from the perspective of a passenger, the following eyewitness account as published in the Toronto Globe (September 2, 1875) is provided. "Passenger's statement, August 27, 1875. I was on deck most of the evening. The weather was beautiful and the stars shone brightly. A steamer was sighted after passing Whitefish Point, showing her green light full starboard side. The steamer proved to be the COMET, and loaded with silver and iron ore, approaching us from the N.N.W. When within a short distance of the MANITOBA the COMET suddenly shifted her course, shutting out her green light and showing her red light, and crossing the MANITOBA's bows. Neither boat whistled; if they had, I should certainly have heard it, I heard the bells in the engine room of the MANITOBA ring. The mate of the MANITOBA was in charge. Just before the collision Captain Symes came on deck, and seeing the positions of the steamers, he jumped with lightning speed into the rigging to ascend to the pilothouse, but ere any orders could have been executed the steamers collided with a fearful crash; the MANITOBA striking the COMET near the forecastle, and cutting into her from twelve to fifteen feet. The COMET then swung round, and the steamers came together with a heavy crash, the water rushing into the COMET through the breach at a rapid rate. The hull of the COMET parted and sank almost immediately. The upper works appeared to crumble and float away from the collision till she sank from sight, it being less than one minute. The mate and crew of the MANITOBA had their boats lowered, ready to render assistance to the sufferers, ere the COMET sank; in fact, Capt. Symes, officers, and crew of the MANITOBA acted nobly, and did everything in their power to save the crew of the sinking steamer. Six of the crew jumped from the wreck to the decks of the MANITOBA, and boats afterwards picked up four, making ten in all saved. There were six men asleep in the forecastle of the COMET, and it is supposed that they were crushed to death, or so badly injured that they could not make their escape. The first engineer was in bed asleep and went down with the ship; the second engineer went down at his post. One poor fellow jumped from the wreck and caught the sash of one of the windows of the MANITOBA, his hold giving way, and falling, was heard to exclaim: "Oh Lord God, I am gone." One poor man was seen to jump but was carried with the suction of the wreck. The other one of the crew that was lost was not seen or heard. The wheelsman of the

MANITOBA was thrown forward over the wheel, and the passengers that were sitting in the saloon were thrown prostrate, and the lamps were put out, such was the force of the concussion.

"His Lordship the Bishop of Moosonee, and the Rev. Dixon, Methodist minister of Sarnia were just preparing to hold evening service in the time of the accident, and ere they had time to gain the deck the wreck had disappeared.

"There were about fifty cabins, the greater part ladies and several deck passengers on board the MANITOBA. They acted nobly, and particular mention is made of the ladies, who appeared perfectly cool, considering the trying circumstances; not a screech was heard, only anxious enquiries, 'Is there danger?'

"One of the cooks of the MANITOBA became so excited that he jumped on the wreck and barely had time to regain the MANITOBA before it was too late.

"The mate of the MANITOBA states that the green light of the COMET was seen quite full, and that within a short distance of each other the COMET gave a short blast with her whistle and ported her helm, to bring her red light in view, thus bringing the COMET to cross the MANITOBA's bows. He rang the bell to check, but the distance being short the steamers collided ere further orders could be executed."

The COMET was built by Peck and Masters in Cleveland in 1857. Her engine, a direct acting vertical engine, was manufactured by the Cuyahoga Steam Furnace Company, also of Cleveland.

Originally owned by Dean Richmond (New York Central Railroad), she went through a variety of owners until her loss, when she was owned by W.M. Hanna and George W. Chapin of Cleveland.

Both the COMET and her sister ship, the ROCKET, were originally built as pure workhorses without any passenger accommodations. However, during the winter layup of 1859-60, upper deck cabins were added to both.

Bad luck had always seemed to dog the COMET.

In 1865 she was on a reef off Port Washington, Wisconsin (Lake Michigan). August 1869 she rammed and sank the sidewheeler SILVER SPRAY. That October the propeller HUNTER collided with the COMET below Detroit. Both sank as a result but were quickly raised and returned to service.

The COMET was first located in the 1970s by veteran Great Lakes diver Kent Bellrichard of Milwaukee. On June 6, 1980 it was relocated by Tom Farnquist and Bob Nicholls of the Great Lakes Shipwreck Historical Society. They reported the wreck in 240-feet of water. For historical documentation, the Great Lakes Shipwreck Historical Society filmed the wreck extensively.

REFERENCES:

Charlebois, Dr. Peter. STERNWHEELERS AND SIDE-WHEELERS. (Toronto: NC Press, 1978).
Farnquist, Tom. "COMET Encounter". GREAT LAKES SHIPWRECK QUARTERLY, Winter 1980.
Great Lakes Shipwreck Historical Society Archives.
Heyl, Erik. EARLY AMERICAN STEAMERS, Volume 3. (New York: Erik Heyl, 1967).
MARQUETTE MINING JOURNAL. August 28, September 4, 1875.
Wolff, "Canadian Shipwrecks...." op. cit.

VESSEL:	WILLIAM B. OGDEN
LOSS:	Recovered
DATE:	June 19, 1877
TYPE:	Schooner
LOCATION:	Whitefish Point

SYNOPSIS:

Whether as a result of gale or fog, the record is not clear, on June 19, 1877, the 139-foot schooner WILLIAM B. OGDEN stranded on Whitefish Point. She was downbound with iron ore when the accident occurred. Later recovered, salvage costs and damages were estimated at $5,000.

The OGDEN was built in 1857 by J.W. Jones at Black River, Ohio. Later sunk near Oscoda in 1881, she was salvaged and returned to service.

REFERENCES:

Lake Superior Marine Museum Archives. Duluth, Minnesota.
Wells, op. cite.

VESSEL:	**CITY OF NEW YORK**
LOSS:	**Recovered**
DATE:	**June 1877**
TYPE:	**Wooden Propeller**
LOCATION:	**Vermilion Point**

SYNOPSIS:

An accident of which little is known occurred in June 1877 when the 395-ton propeller CITY OF NEW YORK and schooner AMERICA collided near Whitefish Point. To prevent her sinking in deep water, the CITY OF NEW YORK was beached at Vermilion Point. She was later recovered and returned to service. She was built in Cleveland in 1863.

The passenger and freight propeller CITY OF NEW YORK (at right), stranded at Whitefish Point in 1877.

REFERENCES:

Lytle - Holdcamper, op. cit.
Wells, op. cit.

VESSEL:	**SATELLITE**
LOSS:	**Total**
DATE:	**June 21, 1879**
TYPE:	**Towing Tug**
LOCATION:	**West of Whitefish Point**

SYNOPSIS:

This 233-ton tug was upbound with five schooner-barges in tow when she struck a deadhead (floating log) and stove in her planking. She quickly sank. Her crew escaped without injury. The SATELLITE, built in Cleveland in 1864, and owned by H. Strong of Detroit, was a $16,000 loss.

REFERENCES:

Lake Superior Marine Museum Archives. Duluth, Minnesota.
Lytle - Holdcamper, op. cit.
Mansfield, op. cit.
MARQUETTE MINING JOURNAL. November 11, 1887.
Wells, op. cit.

VESSEL:	**LAURA BELL**
LOSS:	**Recovered**
DATE:	**November 20, 1879**
TYPE:	**Schooner**
LOCATION:	**Waiska Bay, Whitefish Bay**

SYNOPSIS:

The cold winds of a November gale spelled trouble for the 133-foot, 269-ton schooner LAURA BELL. When in Whitefish Bay, the schooner's rigging and sails iced up badly and thus unmanageable, she was blown aground in Waiska Bay. The crew reached shore safely and hiked to the Soo the following day. Many of the crew suffered terribly from the cold, frostbite being common. The mate reportedly had two *frozen* hands.

Although thought to be a total loss, the LAURA BELL was later recovered.

REFERENCES:

MARQUETTE MINING JOURNAL. November 29, 1879.
Wells, op. cit.

VESSEL:	**DOT**
LOSS:	**Total**
DATE:	**August 25, 1883**
TYPE:	**Schooner-Barge**
LOCATION:	**Grand Marais**

SYNOPSIS:

While in the tow of the steamer M.M. DRAKE, the 374-ton DOT sprang a leak and sank in deep water off Grand Marais. Both vessels had departed Marquette with iron ore. The crew was rescued without incident. The 17-year old DOT was an estimated loss of $15,000.

Two years before, the DOT, then named the MARY MERRITT, was driven ashore at the Hurricane River, ten miles west of Grand Marais. Initially considered a total loss, she was later salvaged, sold, renamed and returned to service.

REFERENCES:

MARQUETTE MINING JOURNAL.   September 10, 1881, September 1, 1883.
Wells, op. cit.

VESSEL: JOHN M. OSBORNE
LOSS: Total
DATE: July 27, 1884
TYPE: Steam Barge
LOCATION: Whitefish Point

SYNOPSIS:

Fog was the cause of the disastrous collision on July 27, 1884 between the wooden steam barge JOHN M. OSBORNE and steel passenger steamer ALBERTA. THE 178-foot, 891-ton OSBORNE was downbound from Marquette with an ore cargo and the ALBERTA upbound when the tragedy occurred. As was typical of the period, the OSBORNE was towing two schooner-barges, the GEORGE W. DAVIS and THOMAS GAWN.

As the OSBORNE was steaming through the fog she was periodically blowing her whistle to warn other vessels of her approach. Suddenly, the pilothouse crew heard the answering blast of another whistle and it was close!

As reported in the local papers, "the barge blew three whistles, the ALBERTA answering, and checked down to seven miles per hour, but in a moment the OSBORNE appeared under the ALBERTAS bow and the latter struck her midway between the main and mizzen masts on the starboard side, cutting her almost in twain."

The two vessels stayed locked together for a short period, long enough for most of the OSBORNE's crew, including the captain and his wife, to climb aboard the ALBERTA. One of the ALBERTA's passengers courageously jumped to the OSBORNE to help save those crewmen still aboard, including the captain's children. While he was below decks, reportedly assisting the engine room crew, the heavily loaded steamer broke free and took the plunge. Down with her went the brave

41

passenger and three of her crew.

The OSBORNE was built in Marine City, Michigan in 1882, by Morely and Hill. Owned by George F. Cleveland and the Cleveland Iron Mining Company, she was a loss of $85,000. The ALBERTA returned to the Soo and a $12,500 shipyard bill. Owned by the Canadian Pacific Railroad, the ALBERTA was a sister to the ALGOMA of Isle Royale fame. In November of 1885, the ALGOMA crashed into an Isle Royale reef, wrecking with the loss of 45 lives. It was the largest loss of life in Lake Superior shipwreck history.

Although the thick fog was obviously the culprit in the OSBORNE disaster, doubtlessly both vessels were travelling too fast for conditions. It was a problem that would be repeated again and again.

The OSBORNE was located during the summer of 1984 by the combined efforts of the Oddessey Foundation of Lansing, Michigan and the Great Lakes Shipwreck Historical Society. The Oddessey Foundation is an educational organization operating in support of Great Lakes maritime heritage. Reportedly the OSBORNE is nearly intact and a time capsule of an earlier era of Great Lakes maritime history.

REFERENCES:

Great Lakes Shipwreck Historical Society Archives.
Lake Superior Marine Museum Archives. Duluth, Minnesota.
MARQUETTE MINING JOURNAL. July 30, August 1, 2, 4, 9, 11, 31, 1884.
Wells, op. cit.

VESSEL:	MORELY
LOSS:	Recovered
DATE:	November 21, 1884
TYPE:	Steam Barge
LOCATION:	Grand Marais

SYNOPSIS:

The MORELY was enroute from Duluth with a grain cargo when she was blown ashore by a north gale at Lonesome Point, east of Grand Marais. Her crew escaped without injury.

The 181-foot, 869-ton MORELY was thought to be a total loss. Wrecking tugs, however, were quickly on the scene. Working in December's icy winds, the tugs GLADIATOR and A.J. SMITH did their best to free her. Big pumps dewatered the steamer's holds and emptied much of her grain cargo. At one point the MORELY was covered with five inches of ice, making the salvors' work extremely difficult. By the end of December they hadn't been able to free her, so they left the stranded steamer for the winter.

Work started again on April 19, with the MORELY covered with even more ice. After dredging a channel through the sandbar that formed around the wreck during the winter and pumping her out again, the salvors succeeded in pulling her free on May 5th. The battered MORELY was towed into Grand Marais harbor for temporary repairs. The salvors reported her in "bad shape," with several holes in the hull, her rudder shoe and rudder gone and both arches broken. But they still thought that "she is much better than no boat at all."

The salvors' troubles were not yet over. While towing her to Marquette for additional repairs, they became caught in an ice field near Au Sable Point. Finally a south wind blew the ice clear and they were able to proceed. Eventually the MORELY reached

Marquette safely. After a more complete patching she was towed to the lower lakes for a rebuild. By July 1886, she was back in service and renamed the GRAND TRAVERSE.

The MORELY was built in 1879 at Marine City, Michigan. At the time of her 1884 stranding, she was owned by Morely and Hill. She was lost on October 20, 1896 after a collision with the propeller LIVINGSTON off Colchester Shoal in the lower lakes.

REFERENCES:

MARQUETTE MINING JOURNAL. November 29, December 13, 20, 27, 1884, May 16, July 24, 1886. Wells, op. cit.

VESSEL:	**FRANK W. WHEELER**
LOSS:	**Total**
DATE:	**September 29, 1885**
TYPE:	**Schooner-Barge**
LOCATION:	**Off Grand Marais**

SYNOPSIS:

A rather strange loss was that of the 190-foot, 797-ton FRANK W. WHEELER. The schooner-barge was downbound from Two Harbors, Minnesota in tow of the steam-barge KITTIE M. FORBES when she began to leak. There was no apparent reason for the WHEELER's unholy appetite for water. She was only two years old and had no previous history of leaking. Unable to take any effective action to save their vessel, the crew abandoned her shortly before she foundered. Both vessels carried iron ore. She had been built in 1884 in West Bay City, Michigan.

REFERENCES:

Lake Superior Marine Museum Archives. Duluth, Minnesota.
MARQUETTE MINING JOURNAL. October 3, 6, November 13, 1885.

VESSEL:	E.B. HALE, FAYETTE BROWN
LOSS:	Recovered
DATE:	August 30, 1886
TYPE:	Steamer, Schooner-Barge
LOCATION:	Pancake Shoal, Off Whitefish Point

SYNOPSIS:

A thick Whitefish Point fog was the cause of the stranding of the steamer E.B. HALE and her tow the schooner-barge FAYETTE BROWN on Pancake Shoal, northeast of Whitefish Point. Both were downbound with iron ore when they strayed off the shipping lanes. They were freed, but only after dumping part of their ore.

REFERENCES:

MARQUETTE MINING JOURNAL. August 31, 1886.

VESSEL:	**EUREKA**
LOSS:	**Total**
DATE:	**October 20, 1886**
TYPE:	**Schooner-Barge**
LOCATION:	**Off Vermilion Point**

SYNOPSIS:

A very typical loss was that of the 138-foot, 330-ton schooner-barge EUREKA on October 20, 1886. She was downbound with ore from Marquette as one of a string of three vessels in tow of the steamer PRENTICE when disaster struck. During a vicious north'er, the string broke up near Vermilion and the small vessel was soon lost to view. As was common practice, the EUREKA, as well as the other schooner-barges were simply left to tough it out while the steamer sought what shelter she could behind Whitefish Point. With their limited sail capability, these vessels would normally be able to manage well enough until the weather moderated and the steamer would be able to reconnect the towlines. But the EUREKA was never seen again, at least not by the PRENTICE.

The next day the propeller WINSLOW sighted what was thought to have been the EUREKA six miles off Vermilion Point. The crew of the WINSLOW couldn't verify it since all they could see was three feet of a schooner's mast and the bow of a white yawl sticking out of the water. It was thought that the yawl was still secured to a davit, thus it couldn't float free. Without seeing a nameboard, the WINSLOW crew was not certain that both were from the EUREKA, but it seemed likely under the circumstances. All of the EUREKA's crew were lost, thus there were no witnesses. Even though the life-savers carefully patrolled the shore, not a body was ever found.

The EUREKA was built in 1873 at Trenton, Michigan. At the time of her loss, she was owned by Whitney of Detroit.

In June of 1983, Tom Farnquist and Gary Shumbarger of the Great Lakes Shipwreck Historical Society located the EUREKA. Another of Superior's long lost wrecks was discovered.

REFERENCES:

ANNUAL REPORT, UNITED STATES LIFE-SAVING SERVICE, 1887. National Archives and Records Service, Washington, D.C.
GREAT LAKES SHIPWRECK QUARTERLY. Fall, 1983.
MARQUETTE MINING JOURNAL. October 23, 30, 1886.

VESSEL:	**ST. MARIES**
LOSS:	**Recovered**
DATE:	**November 10, 1886**
TYPE:	**Steamer**
LOCATION:	**Deer Park**

SYNOPSIS:

A typical November gale blew the 96-foot, 132-ton passenger and freight steamer ST. MARIES in to the shallows off Deer Park. To prevent his vessel from being beaten to pieces, the captain flooded her down, literally sinking her so she rested firmly on the bottom. The ever alert life-savers at the Deer Park Station removed her crew without trouble. Later the ST. MARIE was pumped out and hauled off without great damage. She had been unloading supplies for the Cooks Lumber Company camp when the gale caught her.

The steamer was built in 1875 at Sugar Island, Michigan by Raines Brothers and Lambert. Owned by L.P. Trempe of the Soo, the steamer was out of service

in 1890, her engines passing to the steamer CITY OF
MARQUETTE.

REFERENCES:

*ANNUAL REPORT, UNITED STATES LIFE-SAVING
SERVICE, 1887, op. cit.*
Duluth Daily Tribune. November 13, 1886.
LAKE SUPERIOR MARINE MUSEUM ARCHIVES.
Duluth, Minnesota.

VESSEL: **NIAGARA**
LOSS: **Total**
DATE: **September 7, 1887**
TYPE: **Schooner-Barge**
LOCATION: **Off Vermilion Point**

SYNOPSIS:

Another schooner-barge tragedy occurred on
September 7, 1887, when the 205-foot, 764-ton NIAGARA
foundered northeast of Vermilion Point. The NIAGARA
was downbound with 1,400-tons of iron ore from Ashland,
Wisconsin in tow of the steamer AUSTRALASIA when
both vessels were overtaken by a strong northwest gale.
Gradually conditions worsened, until they were off
Vermilion Point. There the towline broke and in the
fierce seas, the steamer couldn't reconnect. All the
steamer could do was stand by and watch.

Captain Clements of the NIAGARA tried to set
enough sail to enable him to hold the vessel's head into
the waves, but the howling winds blew out his canvas.
Without sails, the NIAGARA was forced into the trough
of the seas where she was soon rolled on to her beam

ends. Quickly the grasping waves swept over her decks and dismasted the helpless schooner.

With the end in sight, Captain Clements and his crew abandoned the dying vessel in the yawl. Their efforts to escape death were to no avail. Within minutes the small yawl overturned, drowning all within. The number of those lost isn't certain since the records differ as to whether there were nine or ten aboard. The last moments of the NIAGARA are only known because the AUSTRALASIA watched her end. Both the NIAGARA and AUSTRALASIA were part of the Corrigan fleet.

It was initially rumored that Captain Clements had his family aboard with him. However when this was proved false, the owners of the NIAGARA started a public subscription to provide for his wife and five small children.

The NIAGARA was built by Parsons and Humble at Barcelona, New York for the Winslow fleet of Buffalo and launched in September, 1873. At the time, the Winslow vessels primarily traded in grain and consisted of four steamers and 13 schooners. The three masted NIAGARA had a nominal capacity of 55,000 bushels. Brand new, she was valued at $40,000; at the time of loss, $30,000.

In 1883 the NIAGARA was sold to James Corrigan of Cleveland and rebuilt. The Corrigan fleet sailed in the iron ore trade and included 15 to 20 vessels.

The wreck remained undiscovered until 1972 when diver John Steele discovered her in a reported 110-feet of water. Steele filmed the wreck extensively.

A large wooden stocked anchor from the NIAGARA was salvaged in 1975 and donated to Lake Superior State College. It is now on display in front of the Norris Center Physical Education Building.

REFERENCES:

ANNUAL REPORT, UNITED STATES LIFE-SAVING SERVICE, 1888, op. cit.

Gerred, Janice H. "The Wreck of the Schooner NIAGARA". PEOPLE AND PLACES, December 23, 1974.

Great Lakes Shipwreck Historical Society Archives.

Lake Superior Marine Museum Archives. Duluth, Minnesota.

Mansfield, HISTORY OF THE GREAT LAKES, op. cit.

MARQUETTE MINING JOURNAL. September 9, 10, 11, October 21, 22, 1887.

VESSEL: **LAKETON**
LOSS: **Recovered**
DATE: **October 23, 1887**
TYPE: **Wooden Steamer**
LOCATION: **Deer Park**

SYNOPSIS:

The lumber dock at Deer Park was the scene of trouble on October 23, 1887. The small 96-foot, 75-ton steamer LAKETON was unloading supplies for nearby lumber camps when a northeast squall blew up. Rather than run to the closest shelter, Grand Marais, 18 miles to the west, the LAKETON's captain decided to anchor about three-quarters of a mile offshore and ride the blow out. It was a mistake. Later in the day the winds increased and snow flurries periodically blotted the small steamer from view. When she was visible, the LAKETON was seen to be taking a fearful beating.

About 4:30 p.m. the Deer Park Life-Savers, under the leadership of the legendary Captain Henry J. Cleary, anticipating that the steamer would need help, brought their surfboat down to the beach opposite the LAKETON and watched. Their wait wasn't long. At 8 p.m. the LAKETON's anchor line parted and the steamer headed for the deadly surf breaking on the outer sandbar. When the Life-Savers saw the danger, they quickly launched their surfboat through the crashing waves and rowed for the LAKETON. They reached the steamer just as she fetched up on the bar. Rapidly the seven man crew leaped into the surfboat. The waves were breaking so high that rather than chance turning his heavily loaded surfboat in the prevailing sea conditions, Captain Cleary backed his boat to a safe landing on the beach. Such a difficult maneuver could only have been accomplished with a well disciplined and trained crew. It stands as testimony not only to the ability of Captain Cleary and his crew, but also to the Life-Saving Service that produced them.

Without a doubt the heroic action of the Life-Savers saved the lives of the LAKETON crew. Captain Charles Barnett of the LAKETON, in a formal letter of thanks to the Life-Saving Service, stated that "...seas blowing over my ship. The breakers half filled their boat but the keeper was the coolest man I ever saw."

The Life-Savers stood by ashore all night. Later when the gale blew itself out, they returned to the wreck and salvaged what they could. The LAKETON had sunk on the bar, but later the Life-Savers floated her and towed the vessel to the dock. Eventually she was repaired and returned to service.

REFERENCES:

ANNUAL REPORT, UNITED STATES LIFE-SAVING SERVICE, 1888, op. cit.
MARQUETTE MINING JOURNAL. November 25, 1887.

VESSEL:	**STARUCCA**
LOSS:	**Total**
DATE:	**November 15, 1887**
TYPE:	**Wooden Steamer**
LOCATION:	**Deer Park**

SYNOPSIS:

Like so many other vessels, the 218-foot, 1,313-ton wooden steamer STARUCCA met her end at the hands of a screaming north gale. She was upbound for Duluth from Buffalo when she steamed into one of Superior's worst tantrums. Blinded by thick snow squalls and battered by the powerful waves, she was driven aground on a sandbar about a quarter mile offshore and 12 miles west of Deer Park.

The steamer's captain sent several ashore in the yawl to summon help from the nearest Life-Saving Station. After a harrowing run through the rolling surf the men landed safely on the beach and hiked through the sand to the Deer Park Station.

The Life-Saving crew, under the firm command of Captain Henry J. Cleary, launched their surfboat and made the long pull to the STARUCCA, reaching her about 5 p.m. The steamer's captain decided however to keep his crew aboard and try to save his vessel when the seas moderated. Instead of rowing all the way back to the station, the Life-Savers landed on the beach opposite the wreck to await developments.

By midnight the captain had changed his mind. The storm had increased in fury and the waves were breaking over the steamer's deck cabins. The captain wanted his crew off and off fast! Frantically sounding his whistle, he called for help.

It took three trips for the Life-Savers to remove all of the crew. Each time they had to beach launch and make the hard pull out through the breakers. The small surfboat shipped much water, especially when crossing the intermediate sandbars, but each time she struggled on. When the surfboat landed after the final trip it, as well as the clothing of the Life-Saving crew, was heavily iced over. It was this type of daring rescue, repeated time and time again, that gave the Life-Saving Service its reputation for courage and seamanship. It is a reputation that has never been equalled.

The propeller STARUCCA. In 1887 she wrecked off Deer Park.

K.E. Thro

The crew of the STARUCCA had also suffered from the cold. Many appeared half frozen. The steamer's captain stated that they would not have survived the night aboard the stricken vessel. Without the Life-Savers, they all would have been dead!

Owned by the Lake Superior Transit Company, the STARUCCA was a total loss of $80,000, including $35,000 of her general freight cargo which was later recovered. A good part of the salvage work was accomplished by the hard working Life-Savers. The STARUCCA was comparatively new, having been built in 1875 by the Union Drydock Company of Buffalo.

REFERENCES:

ANNUAL REPORT, UNITED STATES LIFE-SAVING SERVICE, 1888, op. cit.
Gerred, Janice H. *"The Wreck of the STARUCCA."*
INLAND SEAS, Winter 1979.
Lake Superior Marine Museum Archives. Duluth, Minnesota.
MARQUETTE MINING JOURNAL. November 19, 1887.
Wells, op. cit.

VESSEL:	**PACIFIC**
LOSS:	**Total**
DATE:	**November 16, 1887**
TYPE:	**Steam Barge**
LOCATION:	**Deer Park**

SYNOPSIS:

The old adage "when it rains, it pours," was also applicable to the Deer Park Life-Savers. No sooner had Captain Cleary and his crew finished with the STARUCCA wreck than they were called out again. Again they added to the legend of the "storm warriors."

The reason for the second call was the 187-foot, 766-ton steam barge PACIFIC. After loading lumber at the Deer Park dock of the Cook and Wilson Company, she tried to move out into the open lake, but ran aground on a sandbar about 200 yards offshore. The grounding occurred at about 7 p.m. Since the dock was located directly on the beach, the grounding was in full view of the Deer Park Station. The Life-Savers quickly rowed out and checked with the steamer's captain but he didn't think his vessel was in any particular danger and

54

thought he could probably work his way over the bar. If the seas increased, it would be even better since they would help "bounce" the PACIFIC over the bottom. The Life-Savers returned to the station to await events.

By midnight the seas not only increased, but a full north gale was blowing! The stranded steamer was driven sideways on the bar and hammered by the powerful waves. Using his steam whistle, the PACIFIC's captain called for the Life-Savers.

Cleary and his men responded to the signal. Launching their light surfboat, they made a long, tough pull through the breakers to the PACIFIC. By 4 a.m. all 15 of those aboard were safe ashore. Later the Life-Savers returned to remove the ship's dog, left aboard by the crew in the confusion. As in the STARUCCA rescue, both the PACIFIC and Life-Saving crews were half frozen from the cold and wet.

Throughout the 18th the Life-Savers salvaged what they could from PACIFIC. By the 19th she had completely broken up and the beach was littered with her debris.

The Deer Park area in 1887 was a very desolate place, not very much different than today. Since the road to the nearest town, Newberry, 23 miles away as the crow flies, was closed by deep snow drifts, the steamer's crew was forced to walk to the Soo. It was a hike of 140 miles! Overnight stops were made at the Vermilion Point Station, Whitefish Point Light and Bay Mills. All arrived safely with the exception of one woman passenger who elected to spend the long winter with Captain Cleary and his family, rather than attempt the trek.

The PACIFIC was built in 1864 at Cleveland by Peck and Masters for the Buffalo and Cleveland Transportation Company. Together with the steamers ATLANTIC and ARCTIC, the PACIFIC ran a popular passenger and freight route from the lower lakes to Lake Superior through the 1870s. In 1887 she was owned by Cook and Wilson and had earlier been cut down to her lower decks for use in the lumber trade. She was a loss of $22,000.

REFERENCES:

ANNUAL REPORT, UNITED STATES LIFE-SAVING SERVICE, 1888, op. cit.
GREAT LAKES SHIPWRECKS. (Grand Marais, Michigan: Voyageur Press, 1977).
GREAT LAKES SHIPWRECK QUARTERLY. Volume 1, Number 1.
MARQUETTE MINING JOURNAL. November 21, 25, 26, 27, 1887.
Runge Collection. Milwaukee Public Library.
Wells, op. cit.

VESSEL:	**A.C. ADAMS, MONTEREY**
LOSS:	**Recovered**
DATE:	**June 19, 1889**
TYPE:	**Tug, Schooner-Barge**
LOCATION:	**Sandy Island**

SYNOPSIS:

The fog demon struck again on June 19, 1889 when the tug A.C. ADAMS and schooner-barge MONTEREY fetched up on Sandy Island, about 15 miles northeast of Whitefish Point. The MONTEREY, downbound from Marquette with iron ore, was under the tow of the tug when the accident happened. Initially the MONTEREY was thought to be a total loss, but she was later recovered. The ADAMS was salvaged without trouble.

REFERENCES:

MARQUETTE MINING JOURNAL. June 21, 25, 1889.
Wells, op. cit.

VESSEL:	C.J. SHEFFIELD
LOSS:	Total
DATE:	June 19, 1889
TYPE:	Steel Freighter
LOCATION:	Off Whitefish Point

SYNOPSIS:

The same fog that stranded the A.C. ADAMS and MONTEREY also caused the loss of the nearly new steel freighter C.J. SHEFFIELD. The 259-foot, 1,700-ton SHEFFIELD was upbound for Duluth when she was rammed west of Whitefish Point by the new steel freighter NORTH STAR. Striking the SHEFFIELD amidships, the NORTH STAR nearly cut her in two.

The two vessels stayed locked together long enough for the SHEFFIELD's crew to scamper aboard the NORTH STAR. When all were accounted for, the NORTH STAR backed away and the SHEFFIELD took the plunge into an estimated 150 fathoms of water.

The SHEFFIELD, only two years old, was a loss of $175,000. She was owned by Harvey Brown of Cleveland. The NORTH STAR suffered extensive bow damage, but safely arrived at the Soo.

Although fog was the obvious cause of the accident, as was typical both vessels were travelling at what was considered excessive speed.

REFERENCES:

Lake Superior Marine Museum Archives. Duluth, Minnesota.
MARQUETTE MINING JOURNAL. June 20, 22, July 30, 1889.
Wells, op. cit.

VESSEL:	ZACH CHANDLER
LOSS:	Recovered
DATE:	October 1, 1889
TYPE:	Schooner-Barge
LOCATION:	Deer Park

SYNOPSIS:

As the case of the steamer PACIFIC so dramatically proved, using the lumber dock at Deer Park was often a dangerous affair. On October 1, 1889, the 194-foot, 727-ton schooner-barge ZACH CHANDLER was at anchor just offshore from the dock when a sudden but typical northwester blew up. The steamer HURON CITY attempted to pull her to safety, but her engines failed and she was forced to leave the CHANDLER to her own devices.

The wind was gradually blowing the CHANDLER toward shore, dragging her anchors all the way. It was evident however, that the anchors would hold when the vessel reached shallow water and caught in the larger seas, the CHANDLER would be pounded to pieces. Cleverly, her captain released his anchor cables and she quickly went ashore where her crew was able to lower a ladder and reach the beach! Since the CHANDLER was only about one and one-half miles east of Deer Park, the Life-Savers were soon on the scene. The vessel was released the next season.

REFERENCES:

MARQUETTE MINING JOURNAL. October 3, 1889.

VESSEL:	ATLANTA
LOSS:	Total
DATE:	May 4, 1891
TYPE:	Schooner-Barge
LOCATION:	Deer Park

SYNOPSIS:

The loss of the ATLANTA was another typical schooner-barge disaster. The ATLANTA was upbound with coal in tow of the steamer WILHELM on May 4, 1891 when the strain of a northwest gale broke the towline. The break occurred off Deer Park. It was not in itself terribly serious since if the ATLANTA could set some short sails, she could hold her head to and ride out the blow. But the foreboom broke and the sails blew out. blow. But the foreboom broke and the sails blew out. Forced into the trough of the seas, the schooner began to leak badly.

About 20 miles northwest of Crisp Point, shortly before the waterlogged ATLANTA dove for the bottom, the six men and one woman cook of the crew left her in the yawl. Driven by the gusting northwest winds, the small boat and its occupants ended up in the waters just offshore from the Crisp Point Life-Saving Station. The forlorn survivors attempted to run to shore through the surf, but the inexperienced crew made a fatal error. Running a small boat through the crashing breakers is a very special skill, one learned only from long hours of practice. Unfortunately it was a skill the ATLANTA's crew didn't have. As a result of their amateur attempts, the yawl capsized, drowning three of the crew immediately. The rest hung on desperately to the overturned boat.

At the Crisp Point Station the watchman in the lookout tower saw the overturned yawl, but mistook it for a tree trunk. He never saw the men clinging to it. Only when a local resident spotted the boat were the Life-Savers brought into action. Wading into the surf, they hauled two of the crew ashore alive. Five of the seven of the ATLANTA's crew were dead. The watchman who failed to see the overturned yawl was dismissed. The Life-Saving Service would tolerate no mistakes! The 172-foot, 600-ton ATLANTA was a loss of $37,000. She had been built in 1890 at West Bay City by James Davidson.

REFERENCES:

ANNUAL REPORT, UNITED STATES LIFE-SAVING SERVICE, 1892, op. cit.
Lake Superior Marine Museum Archives. Duluth, Minnesota.
MARQUETTE MINING JOURNAL. May 7, 9, 1891.
Wells, op. cit.
Wolff, SHIPWRECKS OF LAKE SUPERIOR. op. cit.

VESSEL:	**FRANK PEREW**
LOSS:	**Total**
DATE:	**September 29, 1891**
TYPE:	**Schooner-Barge**
LOCATION:	**Off Vermilion Point**

SYNOPSIS:

Heavy weather caused the demise of the schooner-barge FRANK PEREW on September 29, 1891. The 174-foot, 524-ton vessel was in tow of the steamer N.K. FAIRBANKS and upbound for Marquette with coal when the towline parted near Grand Marais. The PEREW ran for shelter behind Whitefish Point, but the terrible northwest seas punished her so badly it was evident to all aboard that she wasn't going to make it. At 9 a.m., when whe was about 15 miles northwest of Vermilion Point, Captain Marky and his crew abandoned her in the yawl. Within minutes the PEREW dove for the bottom.

Deciding not to attempt to run ashore through the pounding surf of the infamous "shipwreck coast," the captain tried to bring the yawl to safety around Whitefish Point. But the strong winds and waves blew the boat to Parisienne Island, 13 miles east of the point. In trying to reach the shore of the island, the yawl capsized in the surf and only one of the seven aboard reached the beach alive.

The PEREW was built in 1867 at Cleveland by Quayle and Martin. At the time of loss, she was owned by T. Wilson of Cleveland.

REFERENCES:

ANNUAL REPORT, UNITED STATES LIFE-SAVING SERVICE, 1892.
Lake Superior Marine Museum Archives. Duluth, Minnesota.
MARQUETTE MINING JOURNAL. October 1, 3, 1891.
Wells, op. cit.

VESSEL:	**SAMUEL MATHER**
LOSS:	**Total**
DATE:	**November 22, 1891**
TYPE:	**Wooden Steamer**
LOCATION:	**Whitefish Bay**

SYNOPSIS:

Fog again was the culprit in the November 22, 1891 loss of the 246-foot, 1,576-ton wooden steamer SAMUEL MATHER. The MATHER was downbound in Whitefish Bay about eight miles above Point Iroquois when the upbound 276-foot, 2,186-ton steel package freighter BRAZIL sliced out of the fog and into the starboard side just forward of the stacks. The MATHER was enroute for Buffalo from Duluth with a cargo of 58,000 bushels of wheat. The collision occurred at 3 a.m. The MATHER took about 25 minutes to sink and all of her crew abandoned her safely although all personal gear was lost.

The MATHER was built in Cleveland in 1887 and owned by the Pickands, Mather Company. She was a loss of $110,000. Of the six vessels that carried the name SAMUEL MATHER, two sank. The SAMUEL MATHER lost in 1891 was number one.

The wreck of the 247-foot SAMUEL MATHER (at left) is nearly intact in Whitefish Bay. It is one of the best known examples of a wooden freighter still available for examination. The steamer CITY OF ROME is at right.

K.E. Thro

The wreck is in 195-feet of water and largely intact. Discovered in May 1978 by Bob Smith of Sault Ste. Marie, she has been extensively explored and filmed by the Great Lakes Shipwreck Historical Society. The MATHER is a rare example of a type of freighter that has long since disappeared from the Great Lakes scene.

REFERENCES:

"Divers Uncover Artifacts From the Original MATHER."
THE INTERLAKE LOG, Spring 1979.
Great Lakes Shipwreck Historical Society Archives.
HOUGHTON MINING GAZETTE. July 1, 1978.
MARQUETTE MINING JOURNAL. November 23, 1891.
Wolff, SHIPWRECKS OF LAKE SUPERIOR, op. cit.

VESSEL:	**YOSEMITE**
LOSS:	**Total**
DATE:	**April 30, 1892**
TYPE:	**Wooden Steamer**
LCOATION:	**Whitefish Bay**

SYNOPSIS:

Fire was always a constant danger for wooden vessels. On April 30, 1892, it spelled disaster for the 152-foot, 310-ton wooden steamer YOSEMITE. The steamer was towing the schooner-barges RYAN and GREY OAK in Whitefish Bay when fire broke out aboard. She burned to the water's edge, becoming a total loss.

REFERENCES:

MARQUETTE MINING JOURNAL. May 2, 1982.

VESSEL:	WESTERN RESERVE
LOSS:	Total
DATE:	August 30, 1892
TYPE:	Steel Freighter
LOCATION:	Off Deer Park

SYNOPSIS:

Big steel freighters were not immune to disaster, as evidenced by the tragic August 30, 1892 loss of the 301-foot, 2,392-ton WESTERN RESERVE. The freighter was upbound light (without cargo) for Two Harbors, Minnesota. When she rounded Whitefish Point, a stiff gale was blowing from the northwest, but it was nothing the WESTERN RESERVE should not have been able to handle. She continued to drive on for Two Harbors. Both Captain Albert Myers and Chief Engineer W.H. Seaman were veterans of the lake and used to a little rough water.

The WESTERN RESERVE was nearly new, having been built only two years before by the Cleveland Shipbuilding Company. Already she had set several cargo records. On her last trip to Marquette, August 5, she took aboard 2,608 tons of ore, more than had ever before been loaded from the port.

Along for the trip was her owner, Captain Peter G. Minch, his wife and their ten-year-old son and seven-year-old daughter. Accompanying them was his wife's sister and her nine-year-old daughter. It was intended to be a fine summer cruise.

All went well until about 9 p.m. when the vessel was 35 miles or so northwest of Deer Park. Suddenly there was a violent jolt and shock. The vessel had cracked across her maindeck and was rapidly sinking.

Quickly the orders were passed to abandon her. All 21 of the crew and six passengers boarded two small yawls, one metallic and one wood. Almost immediately the metallic boat capsized. Only one of its occupants

64

was rescued by the wood boat. The others drowned. Minutes later the 19 survivors aboard the remaining yawl watched the WESTERN RESERVE slide beneath the waves. From the crack to the sinking, only ten minutes had passed!

In the prevailing sea conditions all the survivors could do was keep the yawl's bow into the waves and bail. For ten hours they were blown before the furious wind and waves until about 7 a.m., August 31, when they were about a mile off the beach. A quick succession of breakers capsized the boat. Only one man made it to the safety of the shore, Harry Stewart, a wheelsman. It took him two hours to struggle through the surging waves.

When the 301-foot WESTERN RESERVE broke up and sank off Deer Park, 20 of the 21 people aboard went down with her.

Marine Historical Collection,
Milwaukee Public Library

He later stated, "I saw none of the occupants after I started for the shore but the cries of the children, the screams of the women and moaning of the men were terrible for a few moments, then all was silent." After resting on the beach, Stewart walked ten miles to the Deer Park Life-Saving Station where he told the sad story of the disaster.

The Life-Savers patrolled the beach until September 8, and recovered 16 bodies. That of Captain Minch was identified by an engraved watch. Four bodies were eventually shipped to Cleveland, the rest were buried locally.

Booming through the waves, an artist's rendering of the WESTERN RESERVE.

Lake Superior Marine Museum

The WESTERN RESERVE was one of four near identical steel freighters built in 1890 by the Cleveland Shipbuilding Company. Within two months, two of the four, the WESTERN RESERVE and W.H. GILCHER, had sunk under strange circumstances. In the case of the WESTERN RESERVE there was a survivor to tell the tale. In that of the W.H. GILCHER all hands went down with her. The W.H. GILCHER was steaming in northern Lake Michigan with a coal cargo when she sank. Like the WESTERN RESERVE there was a strong gale blowing, but it wasn't anything the vessel should not have been able to handle. The loss was essentially unexplained.

One school of thought held that the cause of the WESTERN RESERVE disaster and perhaps that of the W.H. GILCHER was a brittle steel fracture. There was some discussion that the quality of the steel used wasn't consistent and under the proper conditions of stress as produced by the seas and cargo loading the steel could have failed with cataclysmic results. However, this was only a theory. The exact cause of both disasters has never been determined.

REFERENCES:

ANNUAL REPORT, UNITED STATES LIFE-SAVING SERVICE, 1893, op. cit.

CLEVELAND PLAIN DEALER. September 1, 2, 3, 1892.

LOG OF THE LIFE-SAVING STATION AT DEER PARK, August 30 - September 8, 1892. National Archives and Records Service, Washington, D.C.

LOG OF THE LIGHTHOUSE STATION AT WHITEFISH POINT, August 1892. National Archives and Records Service, Washington, D.C.

MARINE REVIEW. September 15, 1892.

MARQUETTE MINING JOURNAL. September 2, 3, 5, 7, 1892.

Wells, op. cit.

Wright, Richard. FRESHWATER WHALES. (Kent State University Press, 1969).

VESSEL:	VIENNA
LOSS:	Total
DATE:	September 16, 1892
TYPE:	Wooden Steamer
LOCATION:	Whitefish Bay

SYNOPSIS:

Collisions in fog or thick weather can be understood. One in clear weather is much harder to comprehend, but that is exactly what caused the loss of the wooden steamer VIENNA.

On September 16, 1892, the 191-foot, 1,005-ton VIENNA was downbound in Whitefish Bay. Behind her was her tow, the schooner-barge MATTIE C. BELL. Both vessels carried full loads of Marquette Range ore.

Approaching upbound was the wooden steamer NIPIGON towing the schooner-barges MELBOURNE and DELAWARE. Passing signals were exchanged for a normal port to port crossing, but suddenly the NIPIGON turned and rammed the VIENNA hard on her port side.

Immediately both steamers dropped their tows. When the VIENNA lost power, the NIPIGON attempted to haul her into shallow water, but she was too badly damaged. An hour after the collision the VIENNA sank. All of her crew abandoned her safely.

The VIENNA was built in Cleveland by Quale and Martin in 1873 for the Cleveland Transportation Company. She was one of four steamers built for the line, the others being the GENEVA, HAVANA and SPARTA. The small fleet normally ran in the upper lakes iron ore trade. At the time of her loss the VIENNA was owned by the Orient Transportation Company and was a loss of $50,000.

The 191-foot steamer VIENNA was lost in a fog shrouded collision with the steamer NIPIGON.

K.E. Thro

The VIENNA was originally discovered by the U.S. Fisheries R.V. KAHO while setting fishing sampling nets in 1975. She was extensively explored by divers Kent Bellrichard, Dick Race and Tom Farnquist. The wreck is largely intact in 146-feet of water.

REFERENCES:

Great Lakes Shipwreck Historical Society Archives.
Lake Superior Marine Museum Archives. Duluth, Minnesota.
MARQUETTE MINING JOURNAL. September 19, 1892.
Runge Collection. Milwaukee Public Library.
Wells, op. cit.

VESSEL:	**ZACH CHANDLER**
LOSS:	**Total**
DATE:	**October 29, 1892**
TYPE:	**Schooner-Barge**
LOCATION:	**Deer Park**

SYNOPSIS:

The Deer Park Life-Savers were called out for another rescue on October 29, 1892. A full gale was blowing on the lake when the lookout in the station tower sighted a schooner-barge about nine miles to the westward. It was just after dawn and the schooner-barge was under bare poles, with no sails up. More important, she was also being driven toward the breakers at an alarming rate.

The station crew under Captain Frahm quickly loaded their surfboat and beach apparatus into a wagon, hitched up a borrowed team of horses and headed for the beach. The Life-Savers stopped at a point three miles east of the station where long experience, based on her current rent of drift, told them she would strike the offshore sandbar. Right on cue, at 9 a.m., the battered schooner-barge stranded on the bar, about 300 yards from the beach.

Just before she hit, the schooner-barge launched her yawl. As if by a miracle, the small boat safely made the beach with five of her crew, including the woman cook. Another three people, including the captain and mate were still aboard.

The Life-Savers planned to use their Lyle gun to fire a line from the shore over one of the vessel's masts. Using the line as a base, a breeches buoy would be rigged and one by one the remaining crew would be hauled ashore. But before the line could be fired, the masts tumbled into the boiling water. Without the height of a mast to hold the line high above the waves, the breeches buoy couldn't be used.

Before the Life-Savers could launch their surfboat, the three men left aboard the vessel leaped onto a hastily made raft in a desperate effort to reach shore before the vessel broke up completely. But instead of drifting directly ashore as the men hoped, the capricious currents drove it parallel to the beach. One man, a sailor, was washed off and drowned. A half-mile east the Life-Savers, with life lines attached, were able to wade out into the breakers and drag the two remaining half-dead men ashore.

The vessel turned out to be the 194-foot, 727-ton ZACH CHANDLER. She had departed Ashland, Wisconsin, in tow of the steamer JOHN MITCHELL, with a lumber cargo bound for Cleveland. All went well until the early evening of the 28th when a north gale struck the pair. About 35 miles northwest of Deer Park the towline broke and the CHANDLER was left on her own. Although sails were set in an effort to hold her head to the sea, they soon blew out and helpless, the CHANDLER began to drift before the gale. Her seams opened and she began to flood. It was open to question whether she would sink first or blow on to an offshore sandbar.

The CHANDLER was completely destroyed, a loss of $23,000. She had been built in 1867 at Detroit by James M. Jones. The body of the drowned sailor was discovered about a week later and buried in the sand dunes above the lake.

REFERENCES:

ANNUAL REPORT, UNITED STATES LIFE-SAVING SERVICE, 1893, op. cit.
Lake Superior Marine Museum Archives.   Duluth, Minnesota.
MARQUETTE MINING JOURNAL. October 31, 1892.
Runge Collection. Milwaukee Public Library.
Wolff, THE SHIPWRECKS OF LAKE SUPERIOR, op. cit.

VESSEL:	**N.K. FAIRBANKS**
LOSS:	**Recovered**
DATE:	**August 17, 1893**
TYPE:	**Wooden Steamer**
LOCATION:	**Point Iroquois, Whitefish Bay**

SYNOPSIS:

Captains earn their pay by making decisions and on August 17, 1893 the master of the wooden steamer N.K. FAIRBANKS had to make one. His steamer had inexplicably began to leak, beyond that which his pumps could handle. To save her, he slid her aground off Point Iroquois. Damages amounted to $20,000.

REFERENCES:

ANNUAL REPORT, UNITED STATES LIFE-SAVING SERVICE, 1894, op. cit.
Wells, op. cit.

VESSEL: CHARLES P. MINCH
LOSS: Recovered
DATE: August 29, 1893
TYPE: Schooner
LOCATION: Vermilion Point

SYNOPSIS:

Logging was a major activity along the south coast of Lake Superior and it occasionally caused trouble. On August 29, 1893, the 155-foot, 408-ton, schooner CHARLES P. MINCH struck a log raft with the result that one of the logs stove in the vessel's hull. To prevent her from sinking, the captain ran her ashore near Vermilion Point. After some quick professional salvage work, she was repaired and back in service.

The MINCH was built in 1867 at Vermilion, Ohio, by I.W. NICHOLAS for P. Minch. Later, she was sold to the Gilchrist fleet. Some sources also state she stranded at Crisp Point on August 26, 1896 and was recovered.

REFERENCES:

ANNUAL REPORT, UNITED STATES LIFE-SAVING SERVICE, 1894.

VESSEL: CHARLES J. KERSHAW
LOSS: Recovered
DATE: October 14, 1893
TYPE: Wooden Steamer
LOCATION: Waiska Bay, Whitefish Bay

The wooden steamer CHARLES J. KERSHAW, pictured entering the harbor at Conneaut, Ohio, stranded in Waiska Bay on October 14, 1893. Recovered, she would wreck at Marquette less than two years later.

Marquette Maritime Museum

SYNOPSIS:

The 233-foot, 1,324-ton wooden steamer was downbound when a fierce gale stranded her fast on a reef near Waiska Bay. After lightering some ore cargo, the KERSHAW was released with $5,200 in damages. A bare two years later, on September 29, 1895, the KERSHAW would become a total loss after striking the Chocolay Reef, east of Marquette.

REFERENCES:

ANNUAL REPORT, UNITED STATES LIFE-SAVING SERVICE, 1894, op. cit.
Wells, op. cit.

VESSEL:	**GEORGE L. COLWELL,**
	D.P. DOBBINS
LOSS:	Recovered
DATE:	October 13, 1894
TYPE:	Wooden Steamer,
	Schooner-Barge
LOCATION:	Deer Park

SYNOPSIS:

The lumber wharf at Deer Park caused additional problems on October 13, 1894, when a sudden north gale caught the wooden steamer GEORGE L. COLWELL and her schooner-barge consort the D.P. DOBBINS both loading lumber at the docks. The gale struck shortly after midnight. The COLWELL tried to move away from the dock, but struck a sandbar, breaking her rudder shoe and tearing loose her rudder. Blown back against the dock, she began to pound hard. The crew leaped to the pier and safety. At 3 a.m. the steamer drifted away from the wharf and blew on the beach.

The DOBBINS, still moored to the dock, was also pounding badly but her crew stayed with her until about 5 a.m., when a series of waves swept over her deck. Seeing no reason to risk death, they quickly deserted her. At 9 a.m. she broke loose and went ashore east of the dock.

Both vessels were recovered through the efforts of the wrecking tug MARTIN SWAIN and the Deer Park Life-Savers. The COLWELL was hauled off the beach on the 21st and DOBBINS on the 22nd. Damages to the COLWELL were estimated at $15,000.

REFERENCES:

ANNUAL REPORT, UNITED STATES LIFE-SAVING SERVICE, 1895, op. cit.
Wells, op. cit.

VESSEL:	MISSOULA
LOSS:	Total
DATE:	November 22, 1895
TYPE:	Wooden Steamer
LOCATION:	Off Whitefish Point

The big wooden steamer MISSOULA foundered about 15 miles northwest of Whitefish Point.

SYNOPSIS:

Not only did vessels have to contend with the unexpected difficulties of weather, storm and fog, but there were also the mechanical problems to consider. On November 1, 1895, the 272-foot, 1,926-ton wooden steamer MISSOULA was downbound with grain from Duluth when she broke her drive shaft 30 miles west of Whitefish Point. For a day she drifted, driven southeastward by a gusting northwest gale. Finally, about 15 miles northwest of Whitefish Point she foundered. Shortly before she went, the crew abandoned her in the yawl. A switch in the wind however, blew the small yawl a long, cold 30 miles northeast to Lizard Island where the crew managed to land safely. Borrowing a sailboat, five of the survivors sailed to the Soo, arriving on November 8. The MISSOULA was a loss of $90,000, not including the cargo of 75,000 bushels of wheat. She was built in 1897 in Cleveland and owned by Thomas Wilson of Cleveland.

REFERENCES:

Lake Superior Marine Museum Archives. Duluth, Minnesota.
MARQUETTE MINING JOURNAL. November 9, 1895.
Wells, op. cit.

VESSEL:	DREAM
LOSS:	Recovered
DATE:	July 13, 1896
TYPE:	Yacht
LOCATION:	Deer Park

SYNOPSIS:

This small yacht was anchored opposite the Deer Park Life-Saving Station when a sudden north squall caused her anchor line to part. The DREAM was blown ashore by the gusts. The Life-Savers quickly set out steadying lines to prevent major damage and after unloading three tons of ballast, hauled her off the beach five days later using ground tackle.

REFERENCES:

ANNUAL REPORT, UNITED STATES LIFE-SAVING SERVICE, 1897, op. cit.

VESSEL: **MOUNTEAGLE**
LOSS: **Recovered**
DATE: **July 27, 1896**
TYPE: **Steamer**
LOCATION: **Vermilion Point**

SYNOPSIS:

As a result of a dense fog the steamer MOUNTEAGLE stranded one mile east of the Vermilion Life-Saving Station at 8 a.m., July 27, 1896. Alerted by her whistle, the Life-Savers responded by giving the captain his position as he requested and later in carrying out a kedge anchor. Using the anchor and her own engine, the steamer slid free without damage.

REFERENCES:

ANNUAL REPORT, UNITED STATES LIFE-SAVING SERVICE, 1896, op. cit.

VESSEL: **SAVELAND,**
                    BYRON WHITAKER
LOSS: **Recovered**
DATE: **July 27, 1896**
TYPE: **Schooner-Barge,**
                    Wooden Steamer
LOCATION: **Vermilion Point**

SYNOPSIS:

While working on the MOUNTEAGLE, the Vermilion

Life-Saving crew heard the whistle blasts of another vessel further to the east. As soon as possible the Life-Savers responded, discovering the steamer BYRON WHITAKER and her tow, the SAVELAND, both aground. After arranging to telegraph for tugs, the Life-Savers obtained the services of the local steamer CITY OF GREEN BAY.

The CITY OF GREEN BAY pulled on both vessels for several hours but could budge neither. A tug arrived at 9:30 p.m. and worked all night, finally freeing the schooner-barge at 7 a.m. the next day. The Life-Savers assisted throughout the night, even to the extent of making sail on the SAVELAND.

After freeing the SAVELAND, the tug started to work on the steamer, but the tug's master suddenly took ill. Undaunted, the Life-Saving keeper took charge of the tug. By 11:30 a.m., he had the steamer free.

REFERENCES:

ANNUAL REPORT, UNITED STATES LIFE-SAVING SERVICE, 1897, op. cit.

VESSEL:	**PHINEAS S. MARSH**
LOSS:	**Total**
DATE:	**August 26, 1896**
TYPE:	**Schooner**
LOCATION:	**Crisp Point**

SYNOPSIS:

On August 26, 1896 the 177-foot, 543-ton schooner PHINEAS S. MARSH was downbound from Portage Entry enroute for Buffalo with a cargo of 850 tons of sandstone blocks. Caught in the midst of a fierce north gale, the three masted schooner began to leak. Slowly the MARSH worked her way toward Whitefish Point. With luck she just might make the lee of the point. But luck wasn't with the old schooner.

At 1 a.m. she found herself about five miles west of Crisp Point and a bare half-mile offshore. Her end was near. Crashing waves regularly inundated her decks. Since he knew he was in shoal water, Captain William Somerville ordered his crew into the rigging and began to signal with a coston flare.

At 3:30 a.m. the lookout at the Crisp Point Station sighted the glow of the signal and ran for the keeper, R.M. Small. Just as Small reached the tower a second flare flashed. Immediately Small signaled back with another coston to let those on the wreck know that help was on the way. By 3:45 a.m. Small had launched his big lifeboat and was underway for the wreck.

About two and a half hours later at 6:15 a.m., after a long, tough row through a very heavy sea, the Life-Savers reached the MARSH. As they carefully backed the lifeboat under the stern of the schooner, the vessel rolled heavily to starboard. Then after slowly righting herself and with a death-like struggle, she buried her bow deeply into a heavy sea, took a tremendous lunge to port and went to the bottom, 22 feet below.

Six of the sailors had reached the rigging, but two others and a woman cook were washed overboard and nearly buried by the floating debris. In a moment they would be dead. It appeared impossible for the Life-Savers to reach them quickly enough. The schooner hadn't settled evenly, but was keeled over such that the spars and masts overhung the three victims. Incredibly, the two sailors were able to work their way out of the predicament and reached the comparative safety of the rigging. But the woman cook, burdened by her heavy clothing, was all but lost.

Singing out the commands, "Hold water, port; hard to starboard; now boys, altogether." Captain Small shot the lifeboat clear of the heaviest wreckage and reached the drowning cook. Hauling her aboard, the Life-Savers backed clear.

Panicking, two of the sailors suddenly jumped from the rigging into the lifeboat, injuring one of the Life-Savers. Seeing that the rest of the sailors were getting ready to jump too and knowing that they would swamp the boat, Captain Small pulled away from the wreck. After landing the three survivors on the beach, Small made two more trips out to the wreck, recovering all of the crew.

On August 26, 1896, the schooner PHINEAS S. MARSH wrecked off of Deer Park.

When the Crisp Point crew first landed on the beach they discovered that Captain T.H. McCormick and his Two Hearted River crew were there with their surfboat and beach apparatus. The Two Hearted River beach patrol had sighted the coston signal too. Since the Two Hearted River crew had rented a double team of horses to haul their equipment, they used the team and wagon to carry the survivors to the station for shelter.

The Crisp Point crew left their lifeboat on the beach opposite the wreck and walked back to the station. Later they used the lifeboat to help recover any salvageable items from the MARSH. The survivors of the MARSH were later put aboard a downbound steamer for passage to the Soo.

Built in 1867, at Black River, Ohio, by G.W. Jones, the PHINEAS S. MARSH was a loss of $24,000. She was owned by the Gilchrist fleet.

Captain Somerville of the MARSH was very laudatory towards the Life-Savers. In a letter to the Superintendent of the Service about Captain Small's performance, he stated that, "I can hardly find words to express my feelings for his cool and heroic work in saving me and my whole crew from a watery grave under difficult circumstances".

REFERENCES:

ANNUAL REPORT, UNITED STATES LIFE-SAVING SERVICE, 1897, op. cit.
DETROIT FREE PRESS. August 30, 1896.
DETROIT JOURNAL. September 3, 1896.
Lake Superior Marine Museum Archives. Duluth, Minnesota.
Log of the Life-Saving Station at Two-Hearted River, August 26-29, 1896, op. cit.
Log of the Life-Saving Station at Crisp Point, August 26-29, 1896, op. cit.
Wreck Report, Crisp Point Life-Saving Station, August 26, 1896, op. cit.

VESSEL:	**EBER WARD**
LOSS:	**Recovered**
DATE:	**April 24, 1897**
TYPE:	**Wooden Steamer**
LOCATION:	**Whitefish Point**

SYNOPSIS:

During a thick fog on April 24, 1897 the 213-foot, 1,343-ton wooden steamer EBER WARD ran aground at Whitefish Point at 1:30 a.m. At 7:15 a.m., when the fog cleared some, the Whitefish Point Lightkeeper sighted the steamer and telephoned the Life-Savers at Vermilion Point, ten miles to the west. By 9:45 a.m. the Vermilion Crew was on the scene but was unable to accomplish much. At noon, the Life-Savers heard the fog whistle of a passing steamer, the CITY OF VENICE, rowed out and intercepted her, asking her captain to try to haul the WARD free. Five times the CITY OF VENICE pulled. Four times the cable broke. The fifth time, at 4:30 p.m., the WARD came free.

The WARD sailed for another 12 years, until April 1909, when she struck an ice floe and sank five miles west of the Straits of Mackinac. The steamer was built by F.W. Wheeler of Bay City.

REFERENCES:

ANNUAL REPORT, UNITED STATES LIFE-SAVING SERVICE, 1898, op. cit.
Feltner, Dr. Charles. *"EBER WARD Shipwreck Discovered by Feltners". DIVING TIMES, November/ December 1980.*

VESSEL:	**JOSEPH PAIGE**
LOSS:	**Total**
DATE:	**December 1, 1897**
TYPE:	**Schooner-Barge**
LOCATION:	**Vermilion Point**

SYNOPSIS:

Bundled in warm clothing against the frigid 12 degree temperatures and wearing oil cloths for protection from the spray of the surf, a lone Life-Saver patrolled the desolate beach east of Vermilion Point. On the lake a full north gale was blowing with the waves running perhaps 15 feet high. The roar of the seas breaking on the offshore sandbar could clearly be heard. Periodically thick snow squalls blotted out the world in a swirl of white. The ground was already snow covered and massive 20-foot banks of ice lined the shore. It was simply not a good night to be on the lake!

At 3 a.m. the Life-Saver's sharp eyes spotted something, a flash of light that shouldn't be there! It was the running lights of a vessel and in too close. She would hit the bar! Frantically he signaled her with a coston flare, warning her to turn out to deep water. But it did no good. The unknown vessel struck the bar. Quickly the Life-Saver returned to the station for help.

Loading the surfboat and beach apparatus on a borrowed sleigh, hitching up a borrowed team, the station crew, headed by Captain Bernier, struck off for the wreck. They arrived on the scene just before dawn. At first they tried to fire a line to the wreck with the Lyle gun, but the combination of north wind and distance prevented it. Try as they might, the line kept falling short. The Life-Saver's only hope was to launch the surfboat but the high ice banks meant there was virtually no beach to launch from and the surf crashing into the ice banks made any attempt to manhandle the surfboat into the water virtually impossible. But not completely impossible, not for the "Storm Warriors."

Since more skilled manpower was needed, Captain Bernier called for help from the Crisp Point Station, five miles to the west. Working together, both crews literally lifted the surfboat over the ice banks and into the water. As a result of the spray and crashing waves, their clothing was actually frozen stiff when they finished their difficult task.

At 9 a.m. the first trip to the wreck was made. Due to the freezing weather the doomed schooner-barge was sheeted in ice. As the result of being hammered relentlessly by the waves, the schooner-barge had broken in two and was rapidly being torn apart. The small surfboat was swept by the waves and its crew drenched by the freezing water, but they returned from the wreck with three of the sailors and the woman cook.

However, in trying to ease the boat against the ice banks to land the survivors, a large wave smashed it hard against the sharp ice, damaging it. Again working together as a well drilled team the two Life-Saving crews manhandled the damaged boat out and replaced it with the Crisp Point boat. Again the Life-Savers worked their way through the boiling water to the wreck and again returned, bringing the five remaining sailors.

Both the schooner-barge crew and the Life-Savers had suffered greatly from the cold and exposure. Frozen clothing had to be cut off rescued and rescuer alike.

The wreck was that of the 190-foot, 625-ton schooner-barge JOESPH PAIGE. The PAIGE, in tow of the steamer H.B. TUTTLE, had left Marquette the day before with iron ore. Lashed by the north gale, the PAIGE broke her towline. Unable to fend for herself her sails froze stiff, the PAIGE became unmanageable. It was only a matter of time before she struck the beach. The PAIGE was a complete loss of $19,500, although some of her rigging was later salvaged.

The PAIGE was built in Milwaukee in 1872 by Wolf and Davidson. At the time of her launching she was considered a very fine vessel. The Milwaukee newspapers reported that "...the noble ship slid off the ways in fine style and took to the water very kindly, riding gracefully as a swan. As she moved off the colors displayed the name JOSEPH PAIGE in honor of one of the owners of the beautiful vessel. The PAIGE is a credit to her builders and long may she cruise as a specimen of their skill in naval architecture and a source of profit to her owners."

REFERENCES:

ANNUAL REPORT, UNITED STATES LIFE-SAVING SERVICE, 1898, op. cit.

Cutler, Elizabeth F. and Hirthe, Walter M. *SIX FITZ-GERALD BROTHERS, LAKE CAPTAINS ALL.* Milwaukee, Wisconsin: Wisconsin Marine Historical Society, 1983.

Lake Superior Marine Museum Archives. Duluth, Minnesota.

MILWAUKEE SENTINEL. April 15, 1872.

Wolff, *SHIPWRECKS OF LAKE SUPERIOR, op. cit.*

VESSEL:	**SERVIA**
LOSS:	**Total**
DATE:	**April 27, 1898**
TYPE:	**Wooden Steamer**
LOCATION:	**Off Whitefish Point**

SYNOPSIS:

The wooden steamer SERVIA was downbound from West Superior with corn on April 26, 1898, when she sighted the steamer ARGONAUT dead in the water. The SERVIA, already towing the schooner-barge FRANK D. EWEN, added the ARGONAUT to her towline and proceeded on for the Soo.

About 15 miles northwest of Whitefish Point a fire broke out in the forward compartment of the SERVIA. The crew fought the blaze, as did the crew of the big Canadian Pacific Railroad steamer ALBERTA. The ALBERTA was in the area and freely gave her aid. But in spite of their combined efforts it was hopeless. The fire could not be extinguished and with a storm coming on, it was evident the SERVIA was doomed.

In the early hours of April 27, the SERVIA was abandoned. At 6 a.m. she sank. The ALBERTA towed both the ARGONAUT and EWEN to safety in Waiska Bay.

The 242-foot, 1,425-ton SERVIA was built in West Bay City, Michigan, by F.W. Wheeler in 1883. A loss of $80,000, she was owned by Hawgood and Avery of Cleveland.

REFERENCES:

Lake Superior Marine Museum Archives. *Duluth, Minnesota.*
Wells, op. cit.
Wolff, SHIPWRECKS OF LAKE SUPERIOR, op. cit.

VESSEL:	**NELSON**
LOSS:	**Total**
DATE:	**May 13, 1899**
TYPE:	**Schooner-Barge**
LOCATION:	**Off Grand Marais**

SYNOPSIS:

The 165-foot, 167-ton NELSON was lost in a tragic May 13, 1899 shipwreck. She and the schooner-barge MARY B. MITCHELL were in the tow of the steamer A. FOLSOM when they were struck by a freezing northwest gale west of Whitefish Point. All were upbound for Hancock, Michigan, with coal. In the heavy weather the NELSON's towline snapped. Although the NELSON was able to set enough sail to hold her head into the seas, she was badly battered by the waves and her decks and rigging were coated with ice.

The captain of the schooner NELSON watched in horror as his wife and child drown before his eyes when the NELSON sank.

When it was certain his vessel was lost, her captain placed his five-man crew as well as his wife and daughter into the yawl. He then stayed aboard to handle the davits. After the yawl was safely launched and secured to the schooner-barge by a bowline, the captain jumped for the wildly bobbing boat but missed and landed in the lake. Surfacing, he saw the NELSON raise her stern high into the air and then plunge quickly for the bottom, dragging the yawl and its helpless occupants down with it by the still attached line. Before his horrified eyes, his wife and daughter as well as his five-man crew drowned. He survived and later floated ashore near Deer Park.

The NELSON was built in 1866 at Milwaukee. At the time of her loss she was valued at approximately

$12,000 and owned by the Mitchell Transportation Company of Bay City.

REFERENCES:

ANNUAL REPORT, UNITED STATES LIFE-SAVING SERVICE, 1900, op. cit.
Beeson, Harvey Childs. *BEESON's INLAND MARINE DIRECTORY. (Chicago: Harvey C. Beeson, 1902).*
Journal of the Lighthouse at Whitefish Point, May 1899, op. cit.
Journal of the Crisp Point Life-Saving Station, May 14-19, 1899, op. cit.
Journal of the Muskallonge Lake Life-Saving Station, May 14-20, 1899, op. cit.
Journal of the Vermilion Point Life-Saving Station, May 14, 1899, op. cit.

VESSEL:	**A.C. KEATING**
LOSS:	**Total**
DATE:	**November 8, 1900**
TYPE:	**Schooner-Barge**
LOCATION:	**Coppermine Point**

SYNOPSIS:

While caught in the midst of a west gale on November 8, 1900, this 138-foot schooner-barge broke her towline to the steamer NEW YORK. The accident occurred about 20 miles west of Whitefish Point. Low on fuel, the steamer was unable to try to reconnect the towline. Driven by the winds, the KEATING ended up on the rocks at Coppermine Point, 40 miles northwest of the Soo. Although the crew reached shore safely, the KEATING was a complete loss.

REFERENCES:

BEESON's, 1901, op. cit.
Runge Collection. Milwaukee Public Library.
Wolff, SHIPWRECKS OF LAKE SUPERIOR, op. cit.

VESSEL:	**ARABIAN**
LOSS:	**Recovered**
DATE:	**November 10, 1900**
TYPE:	**Wooden Steamer**
LOCATION:	**Whitefish Point**

SYNOPSIS:

This 178-foot, 770-ton Canadian steamer was driven ashore in heavy weather eight miles west of Whitefish Point. The Life-Savers removed the crew without incident. Later the vessel was hauled free without undue trouble.

REFERENCES:

Toronto Marine Historical Society. SCANNER. Toronto: Toronto Marine Historical Society, April 1981.

VESSEL:	SAGAMORE
LOSS:	Total
DATE:	July 29, 1901
TYPE:	Whaleback Barge
LOCATION:	Off Point Iroquois.

SYNOPSIS:

A dense Whitefish Bay fog on July 29, 1901, spelled the end of the career of the whaleback barge, SAGAMORE. The 308-foot, 1,601-ton barge was in tow of her normal consort, the 340-foot whaleback steamer, PATHFINDER, at 9 a.m. Both vessels were anchored in the downbound channel just north of Point Iroquois waiting for the fog to clear when the 300 foot steel steamer, NORTHERN QUEEN, shot out of the fog and cut deeply into the starboard side of the SAGAMORE. The barge sank quickly, with the loss of two men, her captain, E.C. Joiner and the steward. The remaining five crewmen leaped to safety aboard the NORTHERN QUEEN.

The SAGAMORE was built in 1892 in West Superior, Wisconsin, by the American Steel Barge Company. She was lost nearly ten years to the day from her July 23, 1892, launching. Both the SAGAMORE and PATH-FINDER were downbound with ore from Duluth to Lake Erie when the disaster occurred. Owned by the Huron Barge Company of Huron, Ohio, she was a loss of $90,000.

The wreck was discovered in 1962 by divers Jack Brosco and Robert McCormick of Sault Ste. Marie. Today the wreck of the SAGAMORE is a popular diving target. Resting in 72-feet of water, she is largely intact.

REFERENCES:

BEESON's, 1902, op. cit.

DAILY MINING GAZETTE (HOUGHTON, MICHIGAN). July 30, 1901.

Great Lakes Shipwrecks Historical Society Archives.

Runge Collection. Milwaukee Public Library.

Sault News-Record (Sault Ste. Marie, Michigan). July 30, August 15, 1901.

Wilterding, John H. McDOUGALL's DREAM, THE AMERICAN WHALEBACK. (Duluth: Lakeside Publications, 1969).

Wolff, SHIPWRECKS OF LAKE SUPERIOR, op. cit.

Between 1888 and 1897, 47 whalebacks were built at West Superior, Wisconsin. They proved a remarkably seaworthy design.

Marine Historical Collection,
Milwaukee Public Library

VESSEL: M.M. DRAKE, MICHIGAN
LOSS: Total
DATE: October 2, 1901
TYPE: Wooden Steamer,
Schooner-Barge
LOCATION: Vermilion Point

SYNOPSIS:

A unique double loss occurred on October 2, 1901. The steamer M.M. DRAKE was proceeding in heavy weather with the schooner-barge MICHIGAN in tow off Vermilion Point when the MICHIGAN signalled she was filling with water and would soon sink. Captain Nicholson of the DRAKE quickly dropped the towline and ran the steamer alongside the MICHIGAN to allow the crew to jump to' safety. But at the critical moment a large wave slammed both vessels hard together. The shock of the collision toppled the DRAKE's stack and smashed her cabin. Still the MICHIGAN's crew jumped to safety on the DRAKE, or so they thought. With the stack down, the DRAKE's boiler fire lost its draft and the engine soon was powerless. Helpless and drifting before the seas, the steamer was taking aboard large amounts of water. It was evident she too would soon founder.

Seeing the DRAKE's distress signals, the big steel steamers NORTHERN WAVE and CRESCENT CITY ran over to help. Coming alongside, the NORTHERN WAVE took four men off, while the CRESCENT CITY removed the rest. In the excitement of the moment it was thought all were saved. Later it was realized that in the confusion the cook was left aboard. He was the only casualty.

The DRAKE, 201-feet, 1,102-tons, was built in Buffalo in 1882 by the Union Dry Dock Company. She was a reported loss of $35,000. The MICHIGAN, 213 feet,

1,056 tons, was built in Detroit in 1872. She was a loss of $19,000. Both were owned by James Corrigan of Cleveland.

The wreck of the DRAKE was located in 1978 by the Great Lakes Shipwreck Historical Society. The final resting place of another of the Whitefish wrecks has been recorded.

The 201-foot wooden steamer M.M. DRAKE. In attempting to rescue the crew of the sinking MICHIGAN she collided with her causing her own loss.

Marine Historical Collection,
Milwaukee Public Library

REFERENCES:

ANNUAL REPORT, UNITED STATES LIFE-SAVING SERVICE, 1902, op. cit.
BEESON's 1902, op. cit.
GREAT LAKES SHIPWRECK QUARTERLY. Spring 1983.
Lake Superior Marine Museum Archives. Duluth, Minnesota.

Runge Collection. Milwaukee Public Library.
Wolff, Dr. Julius F. Jr. *"Before the Days of Radar: Ship Collisions on Lake Superior". INLAND SEAS, Summer 1969.*

A diver emerges from the boiler of the M.M. DRAKE.

Author's Collection

VESSEL:	**MONTGOMERY**
LOSS:	**Total**
DATE:	**October 19, 1901**
TYPE:	**Schooner-Barge**
LOCATION:	**Crisp Point**

SYNOPSIS:

The schooner-barge MONTGOMERY met her end on October 19, 1901. She was in tow of the steamer LELAND downbound from Ashland for Cleveland with lumber. During heavy weather the old schooner-barge sprang a leak and became water logged. Her bow sank so low in the water that the crew could not move far enough forward to release the tow line. When the deck load of lath went overboard in the seas, it carried away the rigging on the starboard side. The LELAND dropped the towline and came along side the MONTGOMERY, allowing her seven-man crew to jump to safety on the steamer. To avoid being swept overboard, the MONTGOMERY crew had lashed themselves to the top of the aft cabin. The LELAND continued on for the Soo.

The schooner-barge MONTGOMERY was originally built in 1856 as a propeller.

Marine Historical Collection,
Milwaukee Public Library

Blown before a northwest seas, the MONTGOMERY was sighted by the Crisp Point Life-Savers. Since she was heading directly for the breakers, the Life-Savers rowed out to her but discovered her abandoned. Unable to drop her anchors, they could only watch her drift into the surf three miles west of the station.

The breakers soon beat her to pieces. Assisted by the Two-Hearted River Life-Savers, they salvaged what lumber from her cargo and vessel hardware they could.

The 204-foot, 709-ton MONTGOMERY was an old vessel, built in 1856 at Newport, Michigan, by the Ward Shipyard. Originally she was a propeller, but after an 1878 dock fire, she was rebuilt as a tow (schooner) -barge. At the time of her loss, she was owned by the Port Clinton Transportation Company.

REFERENCES:

BEESON's, 1902, op. cit.
Lake Superior Marine Museum Archives. Duluth, Minnesota.
Runge Collection. Milwaukee Public Library.

VESSEL:	**ANNIE M. PETERSON**
LOSS:	**Recovered**
DATE:	**April 7, 1902**
TYPE:	**Schooner-Barge**
LOCATION:	**Vermilion Point**

SYNOPSIS:

During a strong northwest blow on April 7, 1902, the 190-foot, 631-ton, schooner ANNIE M. PETERSON went ashore just west of the Vermilion Point Life-Saving Station. The PETERSON had been cast adrift from her towing steamer. After a week on the beach she was released.

REFERENCES:

Lake Superior Marine Museum Archvies. Duluth, Minnesota.
Runge Collection. Milwaukee Public Library.

VESSEL:	**J.T. HUTCHINSON**
LOSS:	**Recovered**
DATE:	**April 29, 1902**
TYPE:	**Steamer**
LOCATION:	**Two Hearted River**

SYNOPSIS:

This 346-foot, 3,734-ton steamer stranded in heavy weather at 11:30 p.m., April 29, 1902, about three miles east of the Two Hearted River Station. Beach patrols from both the Two Hearted River and Crisp Point Station discovered her almost as soon as she struck and crews from both stations were quickly enroute. Since the seas were running northwest, the Two Hearted River crew was at the steamer first, as the Crisp Point crew had a hard pull against the seas. The steamer reported she was in no danger, so both crews returned to their normal duties. On May 2, after salvage tugs arrived, the steamer was hauled free.

REFERENCES:

ANNUAL REPORT, UNITED STATES LIFE-SAVING SERVICE, 1903, op. cit.

VESSEL:	ADMIRAL
LOSS:	Recovered
DATE:	September 23, 1902
TYPE:	Steamer
LOCATION:	Vermilion Point

SYNOPSIS:

While the crew of the Vermilion Station was practicing with their surfboat, they noticed the 423-foot, 4,651-ton, steamer ADMIRAL ashore about two and one-quarter miles west of the station. The steamer had lost her bearings in a thick fog. Immediately, they went to her assistance. The Life-Savers were able to get a telegram through to the Soo, via Shelldrake and on the 24th, three tugs arrived at the scene. The Life-Savers assisted the salvors by running cables between the steamer and the tugs. Later that day the ADMIRAL came free. The ADMIRAL was nearly new, built in 1899 at Wyandotte, Michigan, by the Detroit Dry Dock Company.

REFERENCES:

ANNUAL REPORT, UNITED STATES LIFE-SAVING SERVICE, 1903, op. cit.
Lake Superior Marine Museum Archives. Duluth, Minnesota.

VESSEL:	SCRANTON
LOSS:	Recovered
DATE:	September 23, 1902
TYPE:	Steamer
LOCATION:	Crisp Point

SYNOPSIS:

The same fog that the ADMIRAL wandered ashore in, also sent the 268-foot, iron package freighter steamer SCRANTON ashore about two and three-quarters mile east of the Crisp Point Station. The Crisp Point Life-Savers rowed out to the steamer and brought her master to the Vermilion Station where he was able to arrange to send a telegram to the Soo via Shelldrake. Before the tugs from the Soo could arrive, the steamer HUNTER appeared and offered to help. But pull as she might, the HUNTER couldn't haul the SCRANTON free. Early on the morning of the 24th, a northeast sea kicked up and set the SCRANTON moving. With her own power, she was able to back free. Built in 1888 at Cleveland by Cleveland Ship Building Company, she was scrapped in Duluth in 1957.

REFERENCES:

ANNUAL REPORT, UNITED STATES LIFE-SAVING SERVICE, 1903, op. cit.
Lake Superior Marine Museum Archives. Duluth, Minnesota.

VESSEL:	**BARGE NO. 129**
LOSS:	**Total**
DATE:	**October 13, 1902**
TYPE:	**Whaleback Barge**
LOCATION:	**Off Vermilion Point**

SYNOPSIS:

The Pittsburg steamer MAUNALOA and her tow, the whaleback barge No. 129, were downbound with iron ore off Vermilion Point when the towline parted in heavy weather. As the steamer came about to try

100

to pick up the tow, her bow struck the barge and stove in her side. The barge was doomed and sank in an estimated 125 feet of water. The crew escaped to the steamer. Built in West Superior, Wisconsin, by the American Steel Barge Company, No. 129 was 292-feet in length and 1,310-tons gross. She was a loss of $65,000.

Like the SAGAMORE, Whaleback Barge No. 129 was a victim of collision.

K.E. Thro

REFERENCES:

BEESON's, 1903, op. cit.
Dowling, Edward J., S.J. "The Tin Stackers, the Story of the Ships of the Pittsburg Steamship Company".
INLAND SEAS, Winter 1953.
DULUTH NEWS-TRIBUNE. October 15, 1902.
Wilterding, McDOUGALL's Dream, op. cit.

VESSEL:	**W.T. CHAPPELL**
LOSS:	Total
DATE:	October 24, 1902
TYPE:	Schooner
LOCATION:	Vermilion Point

SYNOPSIS:

On October 21, 1902, a fierce southwest squall forced the small two masted 72-foot, 40-ton schooner, W.T. CHAPPELL to come to a quick anchor off Grand Marais. The squall had carried away her staysail halliards and mainsheet rendering her helpless. The Grand Marais Life-Savers arranged for a tug to haul her into port for repairs.

Three days later the schooner was back in trouble, but this time it was trouble she couldn't escape. She was eastbound with a cargo of wood when she sprang a leak in a strong westerly wind. She sank at 1 p.m., October 24, 1902, in seven and one-half feet of water, four and one-half miles east northeast of Vermilion Station. Since the Vermilion Life-Station Keeper actually witnessed the sinking, the crew were soon on the way, arriving in two hours after a long pull. They rescued both of the schooner's crewmen who were clinging to the main topmast shrouds.

Unable to return to the station because of the strong wind and sea, the Life-Savers continued on to Whitefish Point, miles to the east. There they sheltered for a time until the weather moderated. The crewmen from the CHAPPELL were in bad shape. Both were unable to walk and had to be carried to the Whitefish Point Lighthouse where they were provided with a hot meal. Both recovered but the schooner was a total loss. The small schooner was built in 1877 at Sebewaing, Michigan. When lost, she was owned by W.C. Houghton of Sault Ste. Marie.

REFERENCES:

*ANNUAL REPORT, UNITED STATES LIFE-SAVING
SERVICE, 1903, op. cit.*
*Lake Superior Marine Museum Archives.   Duluth,
Minnesota.*

VESSEL:	No Name
LOSS:	Total
DATE:	October 26, 1902
TYPE:	Scow
LOCATION:	Vermilion Point

SYNOPSIS:

After learning that a scow was adrift on the lake
with a man aboard, the Life-Saving crew from Vermilion
Station went out to search. There was a strong southwest
wind blowing and the night was dark, but fortunately
the Life-Savers found the scow and rescued the man
before he was washed overboard. The scow later broke
up, becoming a total loss.

REFERENCES:

*ANNUAL REPORT, UNITED STATES LIFE-SAVING
SERVICE, 1903, op. cit.*

VESSEL:	CHARLES HEBARD
LOSS:	Total
DATE:	November 29, 1902
TYPE:	Wooden Steamer
LOCATION:	Point Mamainse, Ontario

SYNOPSIS:

The night of November 29, 1902, saw the 184-foot lumber hooker with her tows the schooner-barges ALOHA J.A. FRANCOMB and G.D. WARMINGTON, battling their way through a typical fall gale. The small fleet was enroute from West Superior, Wisconsin, for Lake Erie. Somewhere northwest of Whitefish Point the towline parted and each vessel was strictly on its own.

The 184-foot lumber hooker CHARLES HEBARD. Note the heavy deck load of lumber.

K.E. Thro

104

The schooner-barges managed to weather the blow, but only with extreme difficulty. The HEBARD was a different story. Waterlogged and storm battered, she was blown east until she struck the rocks just off Point Mamainse, 20 miles northwest of Whitefish Point. The crew reached shore safely, but the vessel was a complete loss of $40,000. The HEBARD was owned by Nelson C. Holland of Buffalo and was built in Detroit in 1888.

REFERENCES:

BEESON's, 1903, op. cit.
DAILY NEWS RECORD (SAULT STE. MARIE, MICHIGAN). December 1, 3, 5, 1902.
MARQUETTE MINING JOURNAL. December 2, 1902.
PORTAGE LAKE MINING GAZETTE (HOUGHTON, MICHIGAN). December 2, 3, 1902.
Wells, op. cit.

VESSEL:	**E.M. PECK**
LOSS:	**Recovered**
DATE:	**August 6, 1903**
TYPE:	**Wooden Steamer**
LOCATION:	**Vermilion Point**

SYNOPSIS:

At 7 a.m., August 6, 1902, the American steamer E.M. PECK stranded in a fog eight miles east of the Vermilion Station. After receiving word of the wreck, the Life-Savers were underway with the surfboat at 7:40 a.m., arriving at the scene at 9:15 a.m. Pending the arrival of tugs, the Life-Savers stoodby the steamer. Later in the day the wind increased and northwest seas

105

swept across her decks carrying away the deckhouse and part of the aft cabin, flooded her holds and doused her boiler fires. Serious thought was given to removing the crew, but they stayed aboard.

The following morning the storm moderated and the Life-Savers landed two women passengers from the PECK at Whitefish Point. In the afternoon the crew returned with provisions for the wreck.

Later two salvage tugs arrived from the Soo and the Vermilion crew assisted in rigging pumps and handling lines. At 2 a.m. on the 7th, the tugs hauled the PECK free.

REFERENCES:

ANNUAL REPORT, UNITED STATES LIFE-SAVING SERVICE, 1904, op. cit.

VESSEL:	**A.A. PARKER**
LOSS:	**Total**
DATE:	**September 19, 1903**
TYPE:	**Wooden Steamer**
LOCATION:	**Off Grand Marais**

SYNOPSIS:

Storm stress on September 19, 1903, proved the end of the wooden steamer A.A. PARKER. The 247-foot, 1,660-ton PARKER was downbound with iron ore from Superior, Wisconsin, when she ran dead into a rolling southwester. She kept battling on, heading for White-fish Point, but the going just got tougher and tougher. Waves hammered into the old steamer, sweeping down her open decks. The strain proved too much. She started to spit her caulking and leak. The pumps could not keep up with the deluge of water flooding into her hold.

Storm damaged, the 247-foot steamer A.A. PARKER foundered off Grand Marais.

K.E. Thro

About noon, when he was ten miles off Grand Marais, the captain realized it was only a matter of time before he lost his vessel. He headed for the shore and started blowing his whistle, signaling his plight.

The lookout in the Grand Marais Life-Saving Station tower sighted the PARKER and noted she was clearly in distress. He sounded the alarm. The Life-Savers launched and headed for the stricken steamer. After a rough 50 minute row, they reached her, boarded her and determined she was in imminent danger of foundering.

Since the Life-Savers' surfboat couldn't hold the 17 crewmen on the PARKER, the steamer's yawl was lowered and eight of the crew planned to follow the Life-Savers to shore. The two boats rowed only two miles from the PARKER when the steamer sank bow first.

The return trip to Grand Marais was a hard pull for both boats since they were now rowing directly into the southwest wind. After three hours they still had not made it all the way back. It had only been a 50 minute row out! The crashing waves were punishing both crews, especially the PARKER's, unused to long hours of rowing. When they still had three-quarters of a mile to go, the tug E.M.B.A. came out from the harbor and after taking a line from the PARKER yawl, towed it into Grand Marais. When the Life-Savers were within a quarter mile of shore, the tug J.W. WESCOTT towed them in.

The tug J.W. WESCOTT towed the Life-Savers back to Grand Marais after the PARKER rescue.

Lake Superior Marine Museum

The PARKER was built as the KASOTA in Cleveland in 1884 by Thomas Quayle and Son. After being involved in a serious collision in 1892, she was renamed the A.A. PARKER. Owned by the Gilchrist Transportation Company, she was a loss of $75,000.

The PARKER was the fifth Gilchrist vessel wrecked in 1903. Normally the Gilchrist fleet carried no insurance, preferring to be self-insured. However, in the 1903 season, for the first time, the fleet was fully covered.

REFERENCES:

ANNUAL REPORT, UNITED STATES LIFE-SAVING SERVICE, 1904, op. cit.
DETROIT MARINE HISTORIAN. Journal of the Marine Historical Society of Detroit. May 1982.
Wolff, *SHIPWRECKS OF LAKE SUPERIOR, op. cit.*

VESSEL:	**SAVELAND**
LOSS:	**Total**
DATE:	**October 1, 1903**
TYPE:	**Schooner-Barge**
LOCATION:	**Grand Marais**

SYNOPSIS:

On October 1, 1903 Lake Superior was lashed by a typical fall northwest'er. Caught in the blow was the lumber hooker GETTYSBURG towing the schooner-barges BUFFALO and SAVELAND. The GETTYSBURG tried to bring her charges into the safety of Grand Marais harbor and almost made it. Both the GETTYS-BURG and BUFFALO slipped in, but at the critical moment the towline to the SAVELAND broke and she was blown about a mile eastward where she struck an old set of pilings. The Life-Savers responded rapidly and removed the seven man crew.

The 195-foot, 669-ton SAVELAND was a total loss

of $15,000. She had been built in Milwaukee in 1873 by Wolf and Davidson. Originally she was designed to haul grain. In 1902, apparently after some modification, she started in the lumber trade.

The SAVELAND had an earlier brush with disaster on the shipwreck coast. On July 27, 1896, she was ashore at Vermilion. Quick action by commercial tugs and the Life-Savers saved her.

REFERENCES:

ANNUAL REPORT, UNITED STATES LIFE-SAVING SERVICE, 1904, op. cit.
Lake Superior Marine Museum Archives. Duluth, Minnesota.

VESSEL:	**WILLIAM F. SAUBER**
LOSS:	**Total**
DATE:	**October 26, 1903**
TYPE:	**Wooden Steamer**
LOCATION:	**Off Whitefish Point**

SYNOPSIS:

The 291-foot, 2,053-ton wooden steamer WILLIAM F. SAUBER was downbound with iron ore from Ashland, Wisconsin, when she was overtaken by what one newspaper described as "the worst blow in 25 years." The storm reduced the steamer to a desperate condition. Her seams had opened and she was leaking badly. Huge seas rolled over her decks doing terrible damage. The water in the hold continued to build. It was only a matter of time before she foundered. Perhaps it was a futile gesture, but Captain W.E. Morse flew distress signals.

The 291-foot steamer WILLIAM F. SAUBER. She foundered off Whitefish Point on October 26, 1903.

Author's Collection

But the big 371-foot steel steamer YALE sighted the stricken SAUBER and moved in to help. The YALE maneuvered so that the SAUBER was in her lee, thus partially sheltering her from the northwest seas. Together the two vessels slowly worked their way toward Whitefish Bay. The YALE's help wasn't enough. At 11 p.m. on the 26th, it was evident the SAUBER wasn't going to make it. The YALE moved closer alongside and the crew of the sinking SAUBER began to abandon her. Sliding down a line running down the vessel's side, 15 of the 17 aboard the SAUBER safely reached a yawl sent over by the YALE. One casualty, an oiler from the engine room, was crushed when he was slammed between the yawl and hull of the SAUBER. The other was the captain, who apparently thought he could still nurse her to safety and refused to abandon his vessel. Only minutes later, the frigid water reached the boilers and the SAUBER blew, sinking her almost instantly. She was a total loss of $80,000.

The SAUBER was built in Cleveland in 1891 by the F.W. Wheeler Company. She was one of six near identical sisters, the others being the C.F. BIELMAN, L.R. DOTY, IOSCO, TAMPA and UGANDA. Four of the six ended their careers in shipwreck; the SAUBER off Whitefish Point in 1903; the IOSCO disappearing with all hands off the Huron Islands in 1905; the L.R. DOTY foundering north of Milwaukee with 17 men in 1898 and the UGANDA sinking near the Straits of Mackinac after striking an ice floe in 1913.

REFERENCES:

ANNUAL REPORT, UNITED STATES LIFE-SAVING SERVICE, 1904, op. cit.
DAILY MINING GAZETTE (HOUGHTON, MICHIGAN). October 27, 1903.
DETROIT MARINE HISTORIAN. July 1982.
Lake Superior Marine Museum Archives. Duluth, Minnesota.
Wells, op. cit.

VESSEL:	**MARIPOSA**
LOSS:	**Recovered**
DATE:	**June 25, 1904**
TYPE:	**Wooden Steamer**
LOCATION:	**Vermilion Point**

SYNOPSIS:

At 3:30 a.m., June 25, 1904, the 330-foot, 2,831-ton steamer MARIPOSA ran aground in the fog one and one-half miles west of Vermilion Point. Later in the day another steamer hauled her free.

Built in 1892 at Cleveland by the Globe Iron Works, she was scrapped in Hamilton, Ontario, in 1947.

The steel steamer MARIPOSA. She was briefly ashore at Vermilion Point.

Lake Superior Marine Museum

REFERENCES:

ANNUAL REPORT, UNITED STATES LIFE-SAVING SERVICE, 1905, op. cit.
Lake Superior Marine Museum Archives. Duluth, Minnesota.

VESSEL:	**JOSEPH C. GILCHRIST**
LOSS:	**Recovered**
DATE:	**July 17, 1904**
TYPE:	**Steamer**
LOCATION:	**Crisp Point**

SYNOPSIS:

As a result of thick fog on July 17, 1904, the 416-foot steamer JOSEPH C. GILCHRIST stranded midway between the Two Hearted River and Crisp Point Stations. Both Life-Saving crews assisted by running lines and taking soundings. At 3 p.m. the following day, with the help of a tug and another steamer, the GILCHRIST came free without damage.

Built in 1903 at Lorain, Ohio, by the American Ship Building Company, she was scrapped in Hamilton, Ontario, in 1949.

REFERENCES:

ANNUAL REPORT, UNITED STATES LIFE-SAVING SERVICE, 1905, op. cit.

VESSEL:	**JAY GOULD**
LOSS:	**Recovered**
DATE:	**August 16, 1904**
TYPE:	**Wooden Steamer**
LOCATION:	**Grand Marais**

SYNOPSIS:

A thick fog caused the 214-foot, 997-ton wooden steamer JAY GOULD to run aground one-eighth mile east of the Grand Marais Station at midnight, August 16, 1904. The Life-Savers quickly responded to the steamer's whistle blasts and later assisted in running lines and taking soundings when a local tug was used to haul her free. At the time she was owned by the Lake Michigan and Lake Superior Transportation Company.

The JAY GOULD was built in 1869 at Buffalo, New York, by Taylor and Jewett for the Union Steamboat Line. Originally a passenger and freight propeller, she was cut down and rebuilt as a lumber barge in 1906. On June 17, 1918, she foundered in Lake Erie.

REFERENCES:

Log of the Life-Saving Station at Grand Marais. August 16, 1904, op. cit.
Lake Superior Marine Museum Archives. Duluth, Minnesota.

VESSEL:	**W.S. CROSTHWAITE**
LOSS:	**Total**
DATE:	**November 13, 1904**
TYPE:	**Schooner-Barge**
LOCATION:	**WHITEFISH BAY**

SYNOPSIS:

Fire was the gremlin that caused the loss of the 198-foot, 683-ton schooner-barge W.S. CROSTHWAITE. On the afternoon of November 13, 1904, she was anchored behind Whitefish Point when a fire broke out in her forecastle. Rapidly the flames spread throughout the old vessel. There was no chance of fighting it and the crew was lucky to escape in the yawl. Built at Saginaw, Michigan, in 1873, she was owned by the Gilchrist Transportation Company and a loss of $9,000.

REFERENCES:

BEESON's, 1905, op. cit.

VESSEL:	**WESTERN STAR**
LOSS:	**Recovered**
DATE:	**June 11, 1905**
TYPE:	**Steamer**
LOCATION:	**Vermilion Point**

SYNOPSIS:

About 1 p.m., June 11, 1905, the 416-foot American steamer WESTERN STAR grounded eight miles east of the Vermilion Point Life-Saving Station. Eventually the Lighthouse Tender AMARANTH arrived and pulled her free. The station crew assisted in their surfboat by running lines and transporting crewmen.

REFERENCES:

ANNUAL REPORT, UNITED STATES LIFE-SAVING SERVICE, 1906, op. cit.
Lake Superior Marine Museum Archives. Duluth, Minnesota.

VESSEL:	**SIR HENRY BESSEMER**
LOSS:	**Recovered**
DATE:	**June 13, 1905**
TYPE:	**Steel Freighter**
LOCATION:	**Off Whitefish Point**

SYNOPSIS:

A confusion between passing signals nearly caused disaster for two new steel freighters. On June 13, 1905, the 504-foot SYLVANIA collided with the 413-foot SIR HENRY BESSEMER ripping a 175-foot gash down her side. Luckily the tear was above the waterline and the BESSEMER was also light. Damages to the SYLVANIA came to $10,000 and $40,000 to the BESSE-MER.

REFERENCES:

DULUTH NEWS-TRIBUNE. June 14, 1905.
Wells, op. cit.

VESSEL:	**HARRIET A. HART**
LOSS:	**Total**
DATE:	**June 15, 1905**
TYPE:	**Wooden Steamer**
LOCATION:	**Whitefish Bay**

SYNOPSIS:

On June 15, 1905, another vessel was destroyed

by fire. The 178-foot, 554-ton wooden steamer HARRIET A. HART was upbound when a fire broke out aboard. Unable to beat the flames back, the crew abandoned her in the yawl. They were later picked up by the downbound steamer JUANITA and dropped off at Mackinac Island. Built in 1889 at Saugatuck, Michigan, she was owned by Hart's Steamboat Line of Green Bay. She was a loss of $50,000.

REFERENCES:

DULUTH NEWS-TRIBUNE. June 16, 1905.
Wells, op. cit.

VESSEL:	**V.H. KETCHUM**
LOSS:	**Total**
DATE:	**September 16, 1905**
TYPE:	**Schooner-Barge**
LOCATION:	**Parisienne Island**

SYNOPSIS:

The schooner-barge V.H. KETCHUM was downbound with ore from Duluth for Cleveland on September 16, 1905, when a fire broke out in her aft cabin. She was apparently in tow of the steamer NOTTINGHAM. Immediately, she was headed for the nearest land, Parisienne Island, where she grounded in 23 feet of water.

When it was obvious the crew couldn't extinguish the fire, they tried to abandon her in the yawl. In the confusion, the boat capsized. All nine people aboard were able to swim back to the overturned boat except the woman cook. Weighted down by her long heavy skirts, she was going down for the third time when the KETCHUM's mate reached her. His rescue attempt failed and they both drown.

The V.H. KETCHUM before her disasterous September 16, 1905 fire.

Lake Superior Marine Museum

The 233-foot, 1,669-ton KETCHUM burned to the water's edge and was a complete loss of $12,000. Owned by the Seither Transit Company, she had been built in 1874 at Marine City, Michigan, by David Lester for the Toledo and Saginaw Transportation Company. Originally built as a steamer for the grain, ore and coal trade, she was converted into a schooner-barge in 1904. Her old engines went to the new steamer R.W. ENGLAND, the first vessel ever built by the Great Lakes Engineering Works. She was also the first vessel owned by the famous Pickands, Mather Fleet.

The beautiful capstan cover recovered by divers from the KETCHUM is on display at the Great Lakes Historical Society museum in Vermilion, Ohio. A large steel stocked anchor from the wreck is on display at Lake Superior State College.

REFERENCES:

Cutler and Hirthe, SIX FITZGERALD BROTHERS, op. cit.

DULUTH NEWS-TRIBUNE. September 18, 1905.

Lake Superior Marine Museum Archives. Duluth, Minnesota.

PORTAGE LAKE MINING GAZETTE (HOUGHTON, MICHIGAN). September 19, 1905.

Runge Collection. Milwaukee Public Library.

VESSEL:	**GALATEA, NIRVANA**
LOSS:	**Total**
DATE:	**October 20, 1905**
TYPE;	**Schooner-Barges**
LOCATION:	**Grand Marais**

SYNOPSIS:

During a fierce October 20, 1905 gale the schooner-barges GALATEA and NIRVANA broke away from their tow steamer, the L.L. BARTH. All three vessels were owned by the Hines Lumber Company and upbound from Detroit for Ashland, Wisconsin.

The 176-foot, 610-ton GALATEA was blown ashore one-half mile west of the Grand Marais harbor. The 169-foot, 611-ton NIRVANA, with enough sail set to give her steerage way, tried to enter the Grand Marais harbor, but instead struck the pier, punching a hole in her bow below the waterline. She sank nearby in 18 feet of water. The crew managed to hang on to the stern cabin until the Life-Savers were able to make the rescue. The GALATEA crew was also rescued by the Life-Savers. Each vessel was a loss of $15,000.

The hull of the schooner-barge GALATEA on the beach at Grand Marais.

Lake Superior Marine Museum

The GALATEA was built in 1882 at West Bay City, Michigan, by F.W. Wheeler. Originally, she was rigged with three masts. The NIRVANA, also a West Bay City product, was built in 1890 by James Davidson.

REFERENCES:

ANNUAL REPORT, UNITED STATES LIFE-SAVING SERVICE, 1906, op. cit.
Lake Superior Marine Museum Archives.   Duluth, Minnesota.

121

VESSEL:	**TURRET CROWN**
LOSS:	**Recovered**
DATE:	**November 27, 1906**
TYPE:	**Steel Steamer**
LOCATION:	**Grand Marais**

SYNOPSIS:

At 8:45 p.m., November 27, 1906, the 253-foot, 1,141-ton steel steamer TURRET CROWN went ashore west of the Grand Marais piers as the result of high seas and strong winds. When the Life-Savers rowed out, the captain informed them his vessel was resting easily and she was in no danger. Again the Life-Savers assisted when the wrecking tugs hauled her free on the 29th.

Built in Sunderland, England, the 253-foot steamer TURRET CROWN went on the beach at Grand Marais in 1906.

Marquette Maritime Museum

Why the steamer went aground was a matter of some local speculation. The popular story was that the captain had been on a binge and on sighting the harbor light on the west (starboard) pier, thought it was the light at Grand Marais, Minnesota, which was on the port side. When he steered his course to enter, he went dead aground!

The TURRET CROWN was built in 1895 at Sunderland, England, by W. Doxford and Son. She ended her days when she stranded on Manitoulin Island on November 2, 1924. During World War II she was cut for scrap.

REFERENCES:

ANNUAL REPORT, UNITED STATES LIFE-SAVING SERVICE, 1907, op. cit.
Lake Superior Marine Museum Archives. Duluth, Minnesota.

VESSEL: **BATCHAWANNA**
LOSS: **Total**
DATE: **June 27, 1907**
TYPE: **Wooden Steamer**
LOCATION: **Off Coppermine Point, Ontario**

SYNOPSIS:

Fire destroyed the 209-foot, 674-ton wooden steamer BATCHAWANNA on June 26, 1907. Downbound from Fort William with iron ore, she was discovered on fire off Coppermine Point, 17 miles northwest of Whitefish Point. The crew escaped without injury but the vessel was a complete loss of $35,000. The

BATCHAWANNA was built in 1881 at West Bay City, Michigan. Originally the ROBERT A. PARKER, she was sold Canadian in 1906 and renamed.

REFERENCES:

BEESON's, 1908, op. cit.
Detroit Marine Historian, June 1981, op. cit.

VESSEL:	**ALEXANDER NIMICK**
LOSS:	**Total**
DATE:	**September 20, 1907**
TYPE:	**Wooden Steamer**
LOCATION:	**Whitefish Point**

SYNOPSIS:

Lake Superior has always been moody, going from periods of calm to wild squalls with deceptive speed. Guessing the weather on the lake is always chancy. The 298-foot, 1,968-ton wooden steamer ALEXANDER NIMICK was a victim of a wrong guess.

The NIMICK had locked through the Soo at 11:30 a.m. on September 20, but on rounding Whitefish Point decided the weather was too rough to continue. For the night of the 20th she sheltered behind the point. When it looked like the gale had moderated enough to continue, Captain John Randall rounded the point to continue his voyage. The NIMICK was bound for Duluth with a cargo of 3,000 tons of coal.

Just several hours later, Captain Randall realized just how wrong he was. The northwest gale attacked with a renewed fury. The NIMICK tried to make Grand Island, 80 miles to the west of Whitefish Point, for shelter, but in spite of her relatively powerful 1,200 horsepower engine, she could make no progress. Huge waves slammed into the vessel, burying her under tons of green water. An especially large wave swept the cook overboard to his death.

The NIMICK attempted to return to shelter behind Whitefish Point, but in the seaway her steering gear apparently became disabled. Unmanageable, the steamer was being driven rapidly for the shore. Leaks were started in her hull and the pumps couldn't keep up.

When the helpless NIMICK was off Crisp Point, she signaled the Crisp Point Life-Saving Station with her whistle. Recognizing the danger the steamer was in, the Life-Savers launched their surfboat and headed for the NIMICK, but the NIMICK was drifting fast and the storm waters had washed out her running lights. The Life-Savers lost sight of the dying steamer. Riding the crests of the huge waves, the Life-Savers rowed all the way to Whitefish Point but never found the NIMICK.

At 6:40 p.m. the NIMICK struck the sandbar about one and one-half miles west of the Vermilion Station. Telephoned by the Crisp Point Station, the Vermilion crew was standing by when the NIMICK struck. Although they made several attempts, the Vermilion crew was unable to launch their surfboat due to the tremendous breaker. She was also too far out to reach her with the Lyle gun. The Life-Savers could only watch in horror as the steamer broke up.

The mate of the NIMICK was able to launch one of the yawls. The second had been smashed by the seas. Incredibly the mate was able to maneuver it, with ten of the crew aboard, to a safe landing on shore. Just before the NIMICK broke up, the chief engineer donned a life jacket and leaped into the wild lake. He too made it safely to shore. The five men left aboard were killed when the vessel disintegrated.

The 298-foot wooden steamer ALEXANDER NIMICK came to the end of her days off Vermilion Point.

The ALEXANDER NIMICK was built in 1890 at West Bay City, Michigan, by James Davidson for the American Transportation Company. When wrecked she was owned by the Gilchrist Transportation Company and was a loss of $70,000.

Incidentally, John Randall was not her regular master. Captain Frank Bertrand who normally took the NIMICK out had recently had his license suspended for 30 days by the Steamboat Inspection Service. On September 11, Bertrand had left Buffalo with the NIMICK but was forced to return by heavy weather. In the harbor he collided with the steamer CURRY and as a result, suffered the suspension.

REFERENCES:

ANNUAL REPORT, UNITED STATES LIFE-SAVING SERVICE, 1908, op. cit.

CLEVELAND PLAIN DEALER. September 23, 24, 1907.
DETROIT MARINE HISTORIAN, January 1982, op. cit.
Gerred, Janice H. "The ALEXANDER NIMICK Wreck".
PEOPLE AND PLACES, October 28, 1974.
Lake Superior Marine Museum Archives. Duluth, Minnesota.
Wolff, SHIPWRECKS OF LAKE SUPERIOR, op. cit.

VESSEL:	**CYPRUS**
LOSS:	**Total**
DATE:	**October 11, 1907**
TYPE:	**Steel Steamer**
LOCATION:	**Off Deer Park**

SYNOPSIS:

At 9 a.m. Thursday, October 10, 1907, the 420-foot steel steamer CYPRUS departed Superior, Wisconsin. The big Pickands, Mather steamer was downbound with 7,103 tons of Mesabi ore for the Lackawanna, New York steel mills.

By noon Friday she was 52 miles east of Manitou Island at the tip of the Keweenaw and on course for Whitefish Point. The wind was blowing from the north northwest and a considerable sea was running, but the steamer was booming along at 10 m.p.h.

By late that afternoon the weather had further deteriorated. Now a gale was blowing from the north northwest accompanied by a heavy sea. The CYPRUS was running in the trough of the waves and rolling heavily. Repeatedly, waves would wash over her open deck, flooding over the hatches.

The life raft from the CYPRUS on which the lone survivor reached the shore.

On October 11, 1907, the 420-foot steel steamer CYPRUS rolled over and sank off Deer Park.

As a result of water reaching the cargo hold and a partial shifting of the cargo, she also had a distinct list to port. Instead of counter flooding her starboard ballast tanks to even out the list, or turning into the wind and waves, the CYPRUS continued on course. The weather was certainly bad, but it was nothing that a modern, well built ore carrier shouldn't be able to handle, unless she was in trouble. The CYPRUS was in trouble.

Eventually the CYPRUS turned for the south shore. At 7 p.m. the two lifeboats aft were cleared and prepared for use. The flooding and list continued to increase. By 7:30 p.m. her port rail was under water. Five minutes later the engineer telephoned the captain in the pilothouse, apparently telling him that the water had reached the boiler fires and he was losing power to both the engine and pumps. Turning to the men in the pilothouse Captain F.B. Hyck said, "It's all off now." All the men forward went to the lifeboats aft, except four men, the captain, two mates and a watchman. They elected to try their luck with the small liferaft kept on the forward deck.

The four men stoodby the raft until 7:45 p.m. when, about 18 miles north of Deer Park, the CYPRUS gave a lurch and turned turtle, sending the raft and men into the water. When they surfaced and regained the raft, the CYPRUS was gone. It was that quick! Some shouting was heard from the general direction of the stern, but they couldn't tell if the boats had made it away or not. It didn't seem likely they had.

The four men stayed aboard the raft, being blown all the time southward. Shortly before 2 a.m. it reached the breakers and tumbled. All the men climbed back aboard. Three more times it went over, each time all climbed back aboard. Only 200 feet from the beach, it went over for the fifth time, but only one man was able to regain it. Instead of climbing back on top, he just held on and allowed it to drag him inshore, until the water was shallow enough to walk. Near death from cold and exposure, he staggered to the beach and collapsed.

129

Minutes later, a Life-Saver on patrol from the Deer Park Station found the lone, half-dead survivor, who was only able to stammer out the barest details of the disaster. He was Charles Pitz, the second mate, and all the crew of the CYPRUS were lost. Since Pitz had come ashore only a half mile east of the station, he was able, with the patrolman's help, to reach that shelter. At the station, after being given stimulants and dry clothing, he related the details of the terrible disaster.

The Keeper of the Deer Park Station quickly telephoned the other stations to be on the lookout for additional survivors or bodies. Attempts were made to restore the first several "floaters" they located, but it was soon apparent that as the official wreck report noted, "they were beyond all aid." Later patrols would recover the bodies of 20 of the crew.

Why the CYPRUS sank was never determined. While the gale was a bad one, it wasn't one the CYPRUS couldn't have been able to weather without undue difficulty.

One clue to the loss was provided by Captain H.G. Harbottle of the Pittsburg steamer GEORGE STEPHENSON. The STEPHENSON had a boiler out and was downbound running at about four m.p.h. when the CYPRUS passed him at ten m.p.h. Captain Harbottle noticed the CYPRUS was taking water over his decks and leaving a red wake behind. This meant water was entering the cargo hold, being discolored by the red ore and then being pumped out. It was thought that the water mixed with the ore and caused the cargo to shift, eventually causing her to roll.

It was suspected the water had entered through the new Mulholland hatches. These hatches were a sliding variety, overlapping in sections. Because the only seals were steel on steel, the hatches were not watertight unless a special tarpaulin was fitted. Fitting the tarpaulin was not easy due to the mechanism of the sliding steel cover. The evidence is in dispute whether the CYPRUS had taken the time to fit the tarpaulins. It was common paractice not to bother, unless bad weather was expected.

The most remarkable part of the entire CYPRUS wreck was that she was only 21 days old! She had sunk on her second trip.

The CYPRUS was launched on September 17, 1907, by the American Steamship Company for the Lackawanna Steamship Company. She was one of five identical vessels, the others being the ADRIATIC, HEMLOCK, ODANAH and CALUMET. She was a loss of $250,000.

REFERENCES:

Barry, James P. *WRECKS AND RESCUES OF THE GREAT LAKES.* (LaJolla, California: Howell - North Books, 1981).

CLEVELAND PLAIN DEALER. October 17, 1907.

Havighurst, Walter. *MEN AND IRON.* (New York: World Publishing 1958).

Letter, Albert Ocha to Superintendent, United States Life-Saving Service, October 1907.

Letter, Pickands, Mather Company to Keeper, Two Hearted River Life-Saving Station, October 26, 1907.

Letter, Mr. Charles Pitz to Mr. J.G. Kiak, October 25, 1907.

Marine Review. "Loss of the CYPRUS". Cleveland, October 17, 1907.

MARQUETTE MINING JOURNAL. December 11, 1907.

Van der Linden, Rev. Peter, ed. *GREAT LAKES SHIPS WE REMEMBER.* (Cleveland: Freshwater Press, 1979).

Wreck Report, Steamer *CYPRUS,* Deer Park Life-Saving Station, October 11, 1907, op. cit.

VESSEL: **BENNINGTON**
LOSS: Total
DATE: September 5, 1908
TYPE: Barge
LOCATION: Off Whitefish Point

SYNOPSIS:

While being towed from Port Arthur to the Soo, the 250-ton barge BENNINGTON sank off Whitefish Point on September 5, 1908. Two lives were lost. The barge, owned by the famous Reid Wrecking Company, was built in 1891. The reason for the loss was never fully explained since the weather was considered fair.

REFERENCES:

BEESON's, 1909, op. cit.

VESSEL: **CHAUNCEY HURLBURT**
LOSS: Total
DATE: September 6, 1908
TYPE: Wooden Steamer
LOCATION: Vermilion Point

SYNOPSIS:

An expected north gale on September 6, 1908, proved too much for the old 185-foot, 1,009-ton wooden steamer CHAUNCEY HURLBURT. Towing the schooner-barge CLINT, the steamer was downbound for Toledo, Ohio, from Lake Linden, Michigan, with a cargo of stamp sand from the copper mills. Working in the rolling seas the HURLBURT began to "spit" her caulking and started to leak. Taking no chances, her captain turned her for the nearest land. About a half mile northwest of the Vermilion Station the steamer plowed ashore. Spotted quickly by the Life-Savers, the Vermilion crew responded and removed all 14 of the crew. The HURLBURT was a total loss of $15,000. She had been launched on Thanksgiving 1873, by Simon Langell at St. Clair. At the time, she cost $65,000.

The 185-foot CHAUNCEY HURLBURT. On September 6, 1908, she wrecked on Vermilion Point.

Lake Superior Marine Museum

REFERENCES:

ANNUAL REPORT, UNITES STATES LIFE-SAVING SERVICE, 1909, op. cit.
BEESON's, 1909, op. cit.
Lake Superior Marine Museum Archives. Duluth, Minnesota.
Wells, op. cit.

VESSEL:	**NESHOTO**
LOSS:	**Total**
DATE:	**September 27, 1908**
TYPE:	**Wooden Steamer**
LOCATION:	**Crisp Point**

SYNOPSIS

Fog was an expected danger of sailing the Great Lakes, but at the turn of the century there was another danger; smoke from forest fires often obscured vision, sending vessels into collisions as well as on to sandbars and reefs.

At 10:30 a.m., September 27, 1908, the east beach patrol returned to the Crisp Point Station and reported a steamer aground about two and a half miles away. Immediately Captain James Scott rounded up his crew, launched the surfboat and pulled for the wreck.

When the Life-Savers arrived they discovered it was the 284-foot, 2,255-ton wooden steamer NESHOTO, downbound from Superior, Wisconsin, for Cleveland with 2,822 tons of iron ore.

The NESHOTO was fast aground, out one foot forward. The Life-Savers helped the Steamer's crew to shift cargo from forward to stern. After about 50 tons were moved, all by shovel and wheelbarrow, the Life-Savers ran a kedge anchor off her stern. Using her steam winch on the anchor cable and reversing her engine, the steamer tried to back free but failed. After throwing 23 tons of ore overboard, she tried again, but still stayed fast.

That night the wind and seas kicked up from the northwest and the NESHOTO's captain had the Life-Savers bring part of his 16-man crew ashore for safety. Throughout the night the northwester increased in ferocity. At 6:30 a.m. the captain decided to abandon his vessel. The seas had forced the steamer broadside to the beach and were sweeping over her decks. When the Life-Savers reached the beach with the last boat load of crewmen, they hauled the surfboat high on the sand and left it. Everyone walked back to the station. There the NESHOTO's crew were given a hot meal and warm dry clothing.

The 284-foot steamer NESHOTO ran aground off Crisp Point when she was blinded by smoke from a forest fire. A subsequent gale destroyed her.

Marine Historical Collection,
Milwaukee Public Library

The northwest storm knocked the NESHOTO to pieces. When the weather cleared, nothing of the steamer was left above water.

The NESHOTO was built in 1889 in Cleveland by Thomas Quayle and Sons. At the time of her loss she was owned by the Gilchrist Transportation Company. Vessel and cargo represented a loss of $58,000. The steamer was not insured.

REFERENCES:

ANNUAL REPORT, UNITED STATES LIFE-SAVING SERVICE, 1909, op. cit.
BEESON's, 1909, op. cit.
Runge Collection. Milwaukee Public Library.
Wells, op. cit.
Wreck Report, NESHOTO, Crisp Point Station, September 17, 1908, op. cit.

VESSEL:	**FRONTENAC**
LOSS:	**Recovered**
DATE:	**September 29, 1908**
TYPE:	**Steel Steamer**
LOCATION:	**Parisienne Island**

SYNOPSIS:

The same smoke that sent the NESHOTO ashore was also the cause of the 270-foot FRONTENAC slipping aground off Parisienne Island. It took six days to haul her free and damages came to $20,000, a considerable sum of money.

REFERENCES:

Wells, op. cit.
Wolff, SHIPWRECKS OF LAKE SUPERIOR, op. cit.

VESSEL:	**D.M. CLEMSON**
LOSS:	**Total**
DATE:	**December 1, 1908**
TYPE:	**Steel Steamer**
LOCATION:	**Unknown**

SYNOPSIS:

Lake Superior has a number of examples of vessels that "went missing," or just disappeared. Superior is deep and wide and it wasn't unusual for a vessel to be lost with all hands under conditions that did not reveal the location or cause of loss. The steel steamer D.M. CLEMSON was a case in point.

The CLEMSON was upbound from Lorain, Ohio, for Duluth with a coal cargo when disaster struck. She had locked through the Canadian Soo on the morning of November 30, 1908. At the time, all was normal.

The D.M. CLEMSON, owned by the Provident Steamship Company, was one of the largest vessels on the lakes. Built in 1903 at Superior, Wisconsin, she was 5,531-gross tons, 448-feet in length and had a 57-foot beam. At the time of her launching (and sinking) she represented the highest state of the shipbuilders' art.

After clearing Whitefish Point, the CLEMSON took the more direct south route for Duluth, instead of the longer, but more sheltered north route. The north route hugged the north coast giving better protection from the fall gales. Vessels on the south route were open to the full fury of the predominantly north wind and waves.

Captain Frank B. Chamberlain of the steamer J.H. BROWN locked through the Soo with the CLEMSON but selected the safer north route. Later he recounted his struggle with the storm. "We had gone about 75 miles when we ran into a gale, the worst I have ever seen on the lakes. Our engines were shut down and we drifted for twelve hours. Such a storm I never saw. Good old Lake Superior was rolling over our decks house-high. It was the first test my boat got and I don't think she will ever get another like it. I know now what she can stand." Captain Chamberlain and the BROWN arrived in Duluth two days overdue and heavily encrusted with ice.

A giant by any standards, the 448-foot, 5,531-ton D.M. CLEMSON was built in 1903 at Superior, Wisconsin. When launched she represented the highest state of the shipbuilders art.

The CLEMSON never reached Duluth. On December 3, the steamer ALGONQUIN discovered a wreckage field off Vermilion Point. Soon other vessels found wreckage, including red hatch covers, life-jackets and the top of a pilothouse. No identification as to what vessel it came from could be made.

On December 7, the Life-Savers began to find wreckage on the beach at Crisp Point, Vermilion Point and Two Hearted River. Included was a water barrel with "D.M. CLEMSON" painted on one end as well as several CLEMSON life jackets. The pilothouse was discovered washed ashore the following spring and for many years served as a playhouse for a local camp.

Inspite of an extremely intensive search by the Life-Savers including holding the stations open beyond their official closing date, only two bodies from the 24 men aboard were ever recovered. The hull of the CLEMSON has never been found. She remains one of Lake Superior's "went missing".

Note: A more complete examination of the CLEMSON disaster is in the book *Went Missing*, Avery Color Studios, Au Train, Michigan 49806.

REFERENCES:

ANNUAL REPORT, UNITED STATES LIFE-SAVING SERVICE, 1909, op. cit.
Correspondence, Dr. Julius F. Wolff Jr. to Author, dated July 16, 1984.
DAILY MINING JOURNAL (Marquette, Michigan). May 21, 1909.
DULUTH NEWS-TRIBUNE. September 14, 27, 1905; October 21, 25, December 1, 5-12, 16, 17, 1908.
EVENING NEWS (Sault Ste. Marie, Michigan). September 4-12, 14-22, 1908; January 3, May 18, 1909.
Journal of the Life-Saving Station at Crisp Point, December 6-22, 1908, op. cit.
Journal of the Life-Saving Station at Two Hearted River, December 6-22, 1908, op. cit.
Journal of the Life-Saving Station at Vermilion, December 6-20, 1908, op. cit.

VESSEL:	**AURANIA**
LOSS:	**Total**
DATE:	**April 29, 1909**
TYPE:	**Steel Steamer**
LOCATION:	**Parisienne Island**

SYNOPSIS:

Ice may look very beautiful. In the sparkle of a winter sun it might be thought of as nature's crystal. But it can be a dark crystal and a ship killer. On April 29, 1909, the 352-foot, 3,218-ton steel steamer AURANIA found out how dangerous Lake Superior ice can be.

After locking through the Poe Lock on Sunday, April 25, the AURANIA went as far as Point Aux Pins, where thick pack ice forced her aground. She got off without much trouble and proceeded on to Point Iroquois.

On April 29, 1909, the 352-foot steel steamer AURANIA was crushed by the ice in Whitefish Bay.

K.E. Thro

In the words of Captain Robert C. Pringle, the master of the AURANIA, "A northwest gale set in and we sought shelter. Off Parisienne Island the ice came at us from both sides and it was pretty solid. We got close to Gros Cap and later an east wind opened a crack through which we worked toward Parisienne Island. There we remained until Wednesday evening when a southeast wind set us in farther toward Parisienne Island. There the heaviest ice we had to contend with was encountered. We worked around to the westward when we suddenly encountered another heavy floe. The mate at this time examined the forepeak and found everything in proper condition.

"There we stuck until 7:30 Thursday morning, continually backing and filling. We were working loose nicely when the vessel suddenly rolled down on her beam. Knowing something was wrong, I had the engineer back up full speed. This carried us into the heavy ice again which supported the steamer and gave us enough time to get away with the small boats. The heavy ice had crushed in her plates and she filled rapidly. She sank in thirty fathoms of water.

"Getting on the ice we started westward, where we saw a number of boats. The BARLOW was about three and one-half miles from us and the PEAVY boats about a half mile farther. A Canadian vessel was also in the fleet. With the exception of the BARLOW, no attention was paid to our distress signals, the other boats proceeding down the river. They were in light ice while the BARLOW was fast. Captain White (of the BARLOW) made every effort to get loose and reach us. He watched our little groups of men as they were crossing the ice to him and had everything ready to put off in case anything went wrong with us. We found before we had proceeded far that we couldn't pull all the small boats, so we forsook them except for the little "PEGGY." We had to cross four open stretches before reaching the BARLOW. It took us about two and a half hours to make the trip across the ice. It was honey-combed in places and was dangerous."

Captain Pringle later claimed that the Canadian and two U.S. steamers ignored his distress signals. He stated, "They must have seen the AURANIA listing. Had the BARLOW acted the way those steamers did, we'd be eating pigeons on Parisienne Island just now."

The 504-foot steamer J.H. BARLOW later returned the 20 AURANIA men to the Soo. Owned by the Corrigan fleet, she was built in Chicago by the Chicago Ship Building Company in 1895 and was a loss of $200,000.

It is possible the AURANIA was Captain Pringle's second experience with Lake Superior shipwreck. In September 1895 a Robert Pringle was the master of the steamer CHARLES J.KERSHAW when she wrecked on the Chocolay Reef, east of Marquette.

The wreck was located by John Steele in 1972 at the foot of Parisienne Island. She rests in 450-feet of water.

REFERENCES:

DULUTH EVENING HERALD. May 19, 1909.
DULUTH NEWS-TRIBUNE. May 6, 1909.
Great Lakes Shipwreck Historical Society Archives.
Lake Superior Marine Museum Archives. Duluth, Minnesota.
SAULT STE. MARIE EVENING NEWS. April 30, May 1, 1909.
Wells, op. cit.

VESSEL:	**JOHN B. COWLE**
LOSS:	**Total**
DATE:	**July 12, 1909**
TYPE:	**Steel Steamer**
LOCATION:	**Off Whitefish Point**

SYNOPSIS:

At 5:30 a.m., July 12, 1909, the 420-foot, 4,731-ton steel steamer JOHN B. COWLE was struck broadside by the 504-foot steel steamer ISSAC M. SCOTT. The accident occurred in thick fog just north of Whitefish

Point. The COWLE was downbound with ore from Two Harbors, Minnesota, and the SCOTT upbound and light and on her maiden voyage!

The SCOTT's bow cut 20 feet deep into the COWLE, leaving a massive hole. Within three minutes the COWLE had sunk, taking 14 men down with her, only ten crewmen were saved; three picked up by lines thrown from the SCOTT and seven from the water by a hastily lowered lifeboat from the FRANK H. GOODYEAR, a steamer that witnessed the accident. Some of the crew were perched on top of the steamer's wooden hatch covers. Many of the covers had popped loose when she sank.

The 420-foot steel steamer JOHN B. COWLE was another victim of a Whitefish Bay collision.

K.E. Thro

It was a minor miracle that some of the crew were saved. One was off watch and asleep in his bunk when the collision happened. Quickly he ran up on deck in his underwear, leaving all of his possessions behind.

When the COWLE plunged for the bottom, it sucked him down with her, deeper and deeper until suddenly the suction released and he shot to the surface. Grabbing a floating piece of wreckage, he hung on until he heard a nearby steamer, somewhere out in the fog. Making a piercing whistle with his fingers, he attracted her attention and was rescued. All around him, he could hear yells for help from other survivors. Some were saved. Some were not.

The SCOTT was heavily damaged, with two forward compartments holed. Had she been loaded, it is likely she, too, would have sunk. As it was, she had damages of $30,000. The SCOTT would sail for four more years. During the great storm of November 1913, she was lost in Lake Huron with all hands.

The U.S. Steamboat Inspection Service considered all the facts in the disaster and issued their verdict. Captain Rogers of the COWLE and his pilot had their licenses suspended for a month for violating rule 15 of the laws of navigation, that in a fog a vessel shall not be run faster than a moderate speed. Rogers claimed he had checked down to bare steerage way but the inspectors thought otherwise. The pilot of the SCOTT fared worse. His license was suspended for a year for violating the same rule and failing to signal.

The COWLE was built in 1902 by the Jenks Ship-building Company in Port Huron, Michigan. Owned by the Cowle Transit Company of Cleveland, she was a loss of $285,000. Her 7,023 tons of ore was valued at $25,000 and not insured.

In 1972 the wreck of the COWLE was located in 220 feet of water. Today she is just another of the many Whitefish Point shipwrecks.

REFERENCES:

ANNUAL REPORT, UNITED STATES LIFE-SAVING SERVICE, 1910, op. cit.
DETROIT MARINE HISTORIAN, November 1976, op. cit.

DULUTH EVENING HERALD. July 12, 17, 1909.
Gerred, Janice H. "The Sinking of the COWLE".
INLAND SEAS, Spring 1983.
Lake Superior Marine Museum Archives. Duluth, Minnesota.
Runge Collection. Milwaukee Public Library.
Van der Linden, Rev. Peter, ed. GREAT LAKES SHIPS WE REMEMBER II. (Cleveland: Freshwater Press, 1984).
Wells, op. cit.

VESSEL: **ADELLA SHORES**
LOSS: **Total**
DATE: **May 1, 1909**
TYPE: **Wooden Steamer**
LOCATION: **Unknown**

SYNOPSIS:

Another of the famous "went missing" wrecks in Lake Superior is that of the steamer ADELLA SHORES, lost in a gale on May 1, 1909.

The 195-foot, 734-ton ADELLA SHORES was built in Gibraltar, Michigan, in 1894 for the Shores Lumber Company. After the hull was launched, it was towed to Ashland, Wisconsin, where the Shores Mills were located. It was formally launched and christened in Chequamegon Bay. The new steamer was named after Miss Adella Shores, the daughter of the owner of the Shores Company and evidently the apple of her father's eye. Miss Bessie Shores, a younger daughter, performed the ceremony, but instead of a bottle of "hooch," a bottle of water was used!

The ADELLA SHORES was one of the best looking boats in the lumber trade and at the time of her

145

launching was one of the largest. She was also considered a handy boat and would always go to her Ashland dock without the aid of tugs. Together with her two frequent consorts, the barges CONSTITUTION and MIDDLESEX, the ADELLA SHORES was a familiar sight on Superior.

Painted white, the ADELLA SHORES was one of the best looking of the lumber hookers.

Dossin Great Lakes Museum

In 1898 the Shores Lumber Company sold the steamer to Neff interests and in turn Neff sold her in 1908 to the Manx Transportation Company of Cleveland for $30,000. During this time she continued in the lumber trade without serious incident except for her "sinking" in Duluth Harbor in 1901. The SHORES had struck a log which punched a hole in her bow. After settling in shallow water, she was quickly patched, pumped out, reconditioned and placed back in service.

A close up of the ADELLA SHORES as she is loading
cargo directly from railroad cars shows her cargo
boom in action.

K.E. Thro

A similar accident happened in December 1898 when
the steamer was forcing her way through thick ice
at Manistee, Michigan. After a tough struggle, she
arrived at the dock only to sink to the shallow harbor
bottom as a result of several stove in bow planks. She
was again refloated and repaired without trouble.

On her last trip the ADELLA SHORES locked
through the Soo at 8 a.m., April 29, bound for Duluth
with a cargo of 9,200 barrels of salt. That night
distress calls were reportedly heard at Wellsburg
and other points on Whitefish Bay. The Whitefish
Point Lightkeeper however, neither heard nor saw
anything unusual.

Captain Millen of the big steel steamer DANIEL J.
MORRELL, who passed up with the missing SHORES,
said "I saw her while we were in Whitefish Bay,

Thursday afternoon. She crept along behind several of us, following in our wake through the ice. We cleared Whitefish Point about 7 p.m. and I judge the SHORES was at that time about two miles in our rear. A fierce northeast gale was blowing and constantly getting stronger. In my opinion, the SHORES got a few miles out and found things too tough. She was possibly struck by a big cake of ice which started a leak. Captain Holmes then doubtlessly put about and headed for under the Point. With that gale blowing a bad seas was running over there. He doubtlessly got in the trough and with a leak filling her up, she simply went out from under them."

The first wreckage from the SHORES was discovered on May 7, when a steamer passed through a field between Au Sable and Whitefish Points. Included was a pilothouse, yawl boat and wooden furniture. Other vessels later passed through the same field and confirmed it was from the SHORES.

The wreck of the ADELLA SHORES has never been found. She remains one of the great mysteries of Lake Superior.

Note: A more complete examination of the ADELLA SHORES wreck can be found in *Went Missing*, Avery Color Studios, Au Train, Michigan 49806.

REFERENCES:

ANNUAL REPORT, UNITED STATES LIFE SAVING SERVICE, 1910, op. cit.

DAILY MINING JOURNAL (Marquette, Michigan). May 8, 10, 11, 1909.

DULUTH EVENING HERALD. MAY 8, 12, 20, 21, 1909.

EVENING NEWS (Sault Ste. Marie, Michigan). May 8, 10, 12, 1909.

VESSEL:	DANIEL J. MORRELL
LOSS:	Recovered
DATE:	August 13, 1909
TYPE:	Steel Steamer
LOCATION:	Whitefish Bay

SYNOPSIS:

Fog again was the culprit when on August 13, 1909, two 580-foot steel monsters, the DANIEL J. MORRELL and HENRY PHIPPS "brushed" in Whitefish Bay. The MORRELL suffered $10,000 in damages and the PHIPPS, $5,000. But for the will of the gods, it could have been much, much worse.

The 580-foot DANIEL J. MORRELL. In 1909 she stranded on Whitefish Point. In 1966 she sank with the loss of 28 of 29 men in a Lake Huron storm. This is the last known photograph of her before her tragic loss.

K.E. Thro

149

The DANIEL J. MORRELL is best remembered for her tragic November 1966 sinking in Lake Huron. In the midst of a rolling gale she broke in two, taking 28 of 29 crewmen down with her.

REFERENCES:

Wells, op. cit.

VESSEL:	**CHARLES WESTON**
LOSS:	**Recovered**
DATE:	**November 13, 1909**
TYPE:	**Steel Steamer**
LOCATION:	**Whitefish Bay**

SYNOPSIS:

As the result of poor visibility in a thick snow squall, the 540-foot steel steamer WARD AMES collided with the 549-foot steel steamer CHARLES WESTON. The accident occurred in lower Whitefish Bay. Sorely damaged, the WESTON made for shallow water as rapidly as possible. She reached it and sank firmly to the bottom. The big steamer was recovered but cost amounted to $20,000.

REFERENCES:

Wolff, SHIPWRECKS OF LAKE SUPERIOR, op. cit.

VESSEL:	JOHN MITCHELL
LOSS:	**Total**
DATE:	**July 10, 1911**
TYPE:	**Steel Steamer**
LOCATION:	**Off Whitefish Point**

SYNOPSIS:

The 420-foot steel steamer JOHN MITCHELL was running in fog west of Whitefish Point when disaster struck. She was upbound for Duluth with a coal cargo when shortly after midnight on July 10, 1911, the 354-foot steel steamer WILLIAM HENRY MACK appeared out of the grey mist and rammed the MITCHELL on her port side.

The 346-foot steel steamer WILLIAM HENRY MACK. Note the 20-foot gash in her bow from the collision with the MITCHELL.

K.E. Thro

After a July 10, 1911 collision, the 420-foot JOHN MITCHELL came to rest on the bottom upside down off Whitefish Point. She is still there.

Marine Historical Collection,
Milwaukee Public Library

The force of the impact drove the MITCHELL down by the port side and crumpled the bottom half of the MACK's bow back 20 feet. Luckily the two vessels stayed locked together long enough for the MITCHELL's crew to rig a ladder from vessel to vessel. Using it as a bridge, 25 crewmen crossed before the MITCHELL sank. The MITCHELL stayed afloat for only seven minutes. Six more people escaped in a hastily launched lifeboat. Three men went down with her.

It was fortunate that the MACK was downbound otherwise she, too, would likely have foundered and the loss of life been much higher. As it was she suffered a 20 foot hole in her bow and a very expensive shipyard bill.

The MITCHELL was built in 1907 at St. Clair by the Great Lakes Engineering Works. With a rated capacity of 7,500 tons, she was a loss of $300,000.

The licenses of both masters were revoked for one year as the result of an inquiry by the Steamboat Inspectors. They found that both vessels were running too fast for conditions. This was a common cause of fog collisions.

The MITCHELL was located in 1972 by diver John Steele. The massive steamer rests upside down in 150 feet of water. Penetrating the wreck is very constrained, the only available entry point being a side hatch into the engine room. The bow is buried in the sand up to the main deck.

REFERENCES:

GREAT LAKES SHIPWRECK QUARTERLY. Number 2, Volume 2, Number 3, Volume 1, op. cit.
Lake Superior Marine Museum Archives. Duluth, Minnesota.
MARQUETTE MINING JOURNAL. July 11, 1911.
Runge Collection, Milwaukee Public Library.
Van der Linden, GREAT LAKES SHIPS, op. cit.

VESSEL:	**WILLIAM A. ROGERS**
LOSS:	**Recovered**
DATE:	**September 1, 1912**
TYPE:	**Steel Steamer**
LOCATION:	**Off Whitefish Point**

SYNOPSIS:

In the days before radar, collisions in the fog shrouded waters off Whitefish Point and in Whitefish Bay were common. In a fog on September 1, 1912, the 525-foot steel steamer WILLIAM A. ROGERS, upbound from the Soo ran behind the stern of the tug SECURITY and cut her towline to the Standard Oil Barge No. 96. With way still on her, the barge kept moving and struck the big steamer. The ROGERS was forced to return to the Soo and a $20,000 shipyard bill. The barge was not greatly damaged.

REFERENCES:

Wells, op. cit.

VESSEL:	**ALLEGHENY**
LOSS:	**Total**
DATE:	**June 6, 1913**
TYPE:	**Schooner-Barge**
LOCATION:	**Vermilion Point**

SYNOPSIS

On June 6, 1913, the lumber hooker M.T. GREENE was towing the 187-foot, 664-ton schooner-barge AL-LEGHENY through storm tossed waters west of Whitefish Point. Both vessels carried cargos of lumber loaded at Duluth and Ashland. Due to the stress of the summer gale, the towline broke. Just to complicate matters, a thick fog also enveloped the two vessels.

Driven south by the north wind, the ALLEGHENY stranded on the offshore bar, about a quarter mile west of the Vermilion Life-Saving Station. In trying to keep track of her consort, the GREENE briefly went aground but was able to work herself free.

Alerted by the steamer's whistle, the Life-Savers quickly responded. After launching their motor lifeboat, they searched the outer bar until they located the ALLEGHENY. Since the weather was getting worse, with ever larger waves battering the schooner-barge, the Life-Savers removed all of her crew except for one. The unfortunate sailor washed overboard and drowned.

Although part of the ALLEGHENY's cargo was recovered, the schooner-barge was a total loss. She was not insured but was valued at $7,500. She had been built as a three masted schooner at Erie, Pennsylvania by R. Loomis in 1873.

The schooner-barge ALLEGHENY along side a coal unloading dock. On July 6, 1913, she wrecked off Vermilion Point.

K.E. Thro

REFERENCES:

BEESON's, 1914, op. cit.
Lake Superior Marine Museum Archives.   Duluth, Minnesota.
Runge Collection. Milwaukee Public Library.
Wells, op. cit.

VESSEL:	**J.T. HUTCHINSON,**
	FRED G. HARTWELL
LOSS:	**Recovered**
DATE:	**November 10, 1913**
TYPE:	**Steel Steamers**
LOCATION:	**Point Iroquois**

SYNOPSIS:

The infamous November 1913 Great Lakes hurricane also caused some trouble in Whitefish Bay. The tremendous winds on November 10, blew the 514-foot, 6,623-ton steamer FRED G. HARTWELL aground at the head of Point Iroquois shoals. Downbound with ore the HARTWELL had dropped both anchors and run her engines full to try to keep off the shoals, but without success. She was later released and repaired at a cost of $65,000. The storm also blew the 346-foot, 3,734-ton steamer J.T. HUTCHINSON ashore in the same area. She had also been downbound with ore. The HUTCHINSON was recovered at a cost of $20,000.

Both steamers were extremely lucky. The 525-foot, 6,631-ton steamer HENRY B. SMITH, downbound from Marquette with ore, literally disappeared with all hands! In the Great Lakes as a whole, over 60 ships were wrecked, eleven sinking with all hands. An estimated 250 sailors drowned.

REFERENCES:

Wells, op. cit.

VESSEL:	**MAJOR**
LOSS:	**Recovered**
DATE:	**November 13, 1913**
TYPE:	**Wooden Steamer**
LOCATION:	**Whitefish Point**

SYNOPSIS:

The wooden steamer MAJOR was upbound with coal on November 13, 1913, when the tail end of the great storm nearly destroyed her. The MAJOR was plowing along about 30 miles west of Whitefish Point through the still large seas, when a steam pipe burst causing her to lose all power. Thrown into the trough of the waves, her seams opened and she began to leak. Just when it seemed certain the MAJOR would founder with all of her crew, the big 504-foot steel steamer A.M. BYERS appeared and rescued her crew. The MAJOR was left to sink.

However, there was life left in the old steamer. Three days later the steamer GEORGE BARNUM discovered her still floating and towed the MAJOR into the Soo!

The owners abandoned the MAJOR to the insurance underwriters who in turn sold her to the Great Lakes Transportation Company. She ran in commercial service until 1920 when she was sold and converted into a floating drydock.

The 293-foot, 1,864-ton MAJOR was built in Bay City, Michigan, as the JOHN MITCHELL. In 1902 she was renamed the MAJOR.

REFERENCES:

MARQUETTE MINING JOURNAL. November 17, 1913.
Mills, John M. CANADIAN COASTAL AND INLAND
STEAM VESSELS (1809-1930). (Providence, Rhode

Island: The Steamship Historical Society of America, 1979).
Van der Linden, *GREAT LAKES SHIPS, op. cit.*
Wells, *op. cit.*

VESSEL:	**C.F. CURTIS,**
	ANNIE M. PETERSON,
	SELDEN E. MARVIN
LOSS:	**Total**
DATE:	**November 19, 1914**
TYPE:	**Wooden Steamer,**
	Schooner-Barges
LOCATION:	**Grand Marais,**
	Two Hearted River

SYNOPSIS:

On November 19, 1914, Lake Superior claimed three vessels. The 196-foot wooden steamer C.F. CURTIS, 190-foot schooner-barge ANNIE M. PETERSON and 177-foot schooner-barge SELDEN E. MARVIN were lost with all hands during a roaring northeast gale.

On November 18, the CURTIS, with the PETERSON and MARVIN in tow, departed Baraga, Michigan, downbound for Tonawanda, New York. Baraga was a small lumber town located at the foot of Keweenaw Bay. All three vessels were owned by the Hines Lumber Company and carried full cargos of lumber. On the morning of the 19th a screaming northeaster slammed into the small fleet. Heavy squalls blotted out the world in a whirl of white and made accurate navigation impossible.

The 196-foot lumber hooker C.F. CURTIS. Note the open bridge above the pilothouse as well as the deep gashes in her hull.

Apparently the CURTIS tried to bring the tows into shelter at Grand Marais. During the height of the blow, a steamer's whistle was heard by those ashore, but eventually it passed to the eastward. Although the Grand Marais fog horn was sounding, in the screaming wind it didn't carry far enough to be heard by the steamer.

There was no knowledge that a wreck had occurred until 1 p.m. on November 20, when a local resident arrived at the Grand Marais Life-Saving Station and told Keeper Benjamin Truedell that wreckage and bodies were strewn along the beach east of the station. Using the power lifeboat AUDACITY, the crew searched eastward along the shore. At a point eight miles from the station they discovered the stern post and broken spar of a vessel sticking out of the water about 100 feet offshore. On the beach they located a large field of wreckage, including apparently the nameboard from the PETERSON. Further east were the bodies of five men and one woman, all frozen stiff. The area was beyond the normal range for the beach patrol and out of sight from the lookout tower because of a small point of land.

A full search by the Life-Savers revealed the scope of the tragedy. Further east was the wreckage of the CURTIS and MARVIN and the bodies of the crews. Two sailors from the CURTIS had evidently reached the beach alive, but died from cold and exhaustion. Both had reached the top of a 20-foot high sand dune, but one had slipped and fallen half way down. The other man had continued on, walking and crawling for seven miles until he died at the base of the Grand Marais breakwall.

The schooner-barge ANNIE M. PETERSON. Notice the smoke stack on the foredeck for her donkey steam engine.

K.E. Thro

The bodies of two sisters, both cooks on the CURTIS, were found near Grand Marais. Both wore fur coats and jewelry, so apparently they had time to prepare before abandoning the steamer. It was thought the lifeboats from both the CURTIS and PETERSON had capsized in the surf.

Judging from the wreckage, it was guessed that the CURTIS and PETERSON were blown into the shallow water between Grand Marais and the Two Hearted River. The waves reduced the vessels to splinters. The MARVIN seemed to have struggled on alone. Her wreckage was discovered between the Two-Hearted River and Crisp Point. None of the bodies of the MARVIN crew was ever found.

The schooner-barge SELDEN E. MARVIN, heavily laden with a deck load of lumber.

K.E. Thro

The why of the disaster can only be surmised. But based on prior wrecks, the vessels were simply overwhelmed by the storm. They found themselves in sea conditions they could not handle. Doubtlessly the fact that the steamer CURTIS only had 485 horsepower engine, insufficient to power her and her charges through storm driven waves, played a part.

The 631-ton PETERSON was built as a three masted schooner at Green Bay, Wisconsin, by A. Johnson in 1874. She had originally been owned by the Hebard Lumber interests of Pequaming, Michigan. The 618-ton MARVIN was built in 1881 by Bailey Brothers at Toledo. The 691-ton CURTIS was built at Marine City, Michigan, in 1882 by D. Lester.

REFERENCES:

ANNUAL REPORT, UNITED STATES LIFE-SAVING SERVICE, 1915, op. cit.
BEESON's, 1915, op. cit.
Lake Superior Marine Museum Archives. Duluth, Minnesota.
Log of the Life-Saving Station at Grand Marais, November 1914, op. cit.
Log of the Life-Saving Station at Two Hearted River, November 1914, op. cit.
MARQUETTE MINING JOURNAL. November 21, 22, 23, 24, 28, 30, Decembr 1, 2, 3, 8, 18, 1914.
Norberg, Carl A. "The Race to Buffalo Harbor". TELESCOPE, January-February 1982.
Runge Collection. Milwaukee Public Library.
Sanderson, Herbert J. PICTORIAL MARINE HISTORY. (Sturgeon Bay, Wisconsin, no date).
Wells, op. cit.

VESSEL:	PANTHER
LOSS:	Total
DATE:	June 27, 1916
TYPE:	Wooden Steamer
LOCATION:	Whitefish Bay

SYNOPSIS:

The 237-foot, 1,373-ton wooden steamer PANTHER was downbound with 65,000 bushels of wheat from Fort William when she met her end. In a thick fog, the 478-foot steel steamer JAMES J. HILL rammed her amidships. Wisely, the captain of the HILL kept his bow in the hole long enough for all of the PANTHER's crew to scamper aboard his vessel. When he pulled out, the PANTHER plunged for the bottom.

The PANTHER was built in 1890 at West Bay City by James Davidson. Her single cargo hold had a capacity of 2,100-tons. On May 19, 1916, she was sold by the American Steamship Company, the latest in a series of previous owners, to the Massey Steamship Company of Fort William. It was intended she would run in the grain trade. For the PANTHER it was a short career. She was a loss of $40,000.

The 237-foot wooden steamer PANTHER. She sank in Whitefish Bay after a collision with the steel steamer JAMES J. HILL.

K.E. Thro

The PANTHER was no stranger to shipwreck. On November 21, 1910, she was sunk near Garden. Island, Lake Michigan. Repaired, she ran without trouble until her loss.

The wreck was located in 105-feet of water in 1975 by the U.S. Fisheries R.V. KAHO.

REFERENCES:

BEESON's, 1911, op. cit.
Great Lakes Shipwreck Historical Society Archives.
Lake Superior Marine Museum Archives.   Duluth, Minnesota.
MARQUETTE MINING JOURNAL. June 28, 1916.
Mills, CANADIAN COASTAL AND INLAND, op. cit.
Runge Collection. Milwaukee Public Library.
Winkleman, A. SHIPPING CASUALTIES RESULTING IN TOTAL LOSS ON THE GREAT LAKES (1878-1970). not dated.

VESSEL:	**WILLIAM S. MACK**
LOSS:	**Recovered**
DATE:	**July 9, 1917**
TYPE:	**Steel Steamer**
LOCATION:	**Off Whitefish Point**

SYNOPSIS:

In a thick fog on July 9, 1917, the 346-foot, 3,781-ton freighter WILLIAM S. MACK was rammed by the Canadian passenger steamer MANITOBA. The accident occurred at 4:20 p.m., about two and a half miles, east southeast of Whitefish Point. The MACK was badly damaged, but not fatally. Her captain was able to nurse her into shallow water where his ship settled to the bottom in 20 feet. Repairs cost $20,000. The blame for the collision was placed on the MANITOBA, which was found to have been travelling at "too high a rate of speed."

REFERENCES:

Lake Superior Marine Museum Archives. Duluth, Minnesota.
MARQUETTE MINING JOURNAL. July 10, 1917.
Wells, op. cit.

VESSEL:	CHESTER A CONGDON, GEORGE G. BARNUM
LOSS:	Recovered
DATE:	May 31, 1918
TYPE:	Steel Steamers
LOCATION:	Off Whitefish Point

SYNOPSIS:

While upbound on May 31, 1918, the 532-foot steel steamer CHESTER A CONGDON stranded on the north edge of the Whitefish Point sandbar. The steamer GEORGE G. BARNUM, also upbound, soon slid onto the same bar, striking the CONGDON on her port side. Apparently the CONGDON had misjudged her distance off the Whitefish Point Light and the BARNUM in turn thought the CONGDON was in deep water. Each vessel sustained an estimated $3,000 in damages.

On November 6, 1918, the CONGDON, while downbound from Fort William with wheat, struck a reef southwest of Isle Royale's Canoe Rocks. She was a total loss of $1,000,000.

165

The 532-foot steel steamer **CHESTER A. CONGDON** wrecked at Isle Royale six months after she stranded at Whitefish Point.

REFERENCES:

Wells, op. cit.

VESSEL:	**H.B. RUNNELS**
LOSS:	**Total**
DATE:	**November 14, 1919**
TYPE:	**Wooden Steamer**
LOCATION:	**Grand Marais**

SYNOPSIS:

The rescues performed by the Life-Savers and later the Coast Guard have been "reasonably routine." The storm conditions may have been truly horrible and the courage and bravery of the Life-Saving crews beyond comparison, but at least all of the equipment worked and all of the personnel were healthy. Such was not the case in the wreck of the steamer H.B. RUNNELS. In many respects, this rescue may have been their finest hour.

During the early morning hours of November 14, 1919, a wild northwest storm lashed Lake Superior. Mountainous seas marched across the horizon and a wind born in the bowels of hell swept the beaches. A blizzard of snow obscured vision and drifted shut local roads. Temperatures dropped to the teens. Vessels everywhere battled against the ravages of the wild lake. One was the 178-foot, 889-ton wooden steamer H.B. RUNNELS, upbound with coal from Lake Erie for Lake Linden on the Keweenaw.

The RUNNELS adventure began at 5:30 a.m., November 14, when Surfman George Olson, atop the Grand Marais Coast Guard Station lookout tower, reported a steamer on the wrong side of the west pier at the harbor entrance. Apparently she was trying to shelter in the harbor. Thinking that if the vessel wasn't in trouble yet, she soon would be, he summoned the crew. Quickly they readied their beach gear and launched the big powered lifeboat. The lifeboat was kept at the dock behind the station, safe in the calm waters of the harbor.

The steamer, however, was seen to back out into the lake and hove to, about one and one-half miles to the north of the station. Since the steamer showed no distress signals, the Coast Guard assumed she would wait until daybreak to enter the harbor. But in any case, they would be prepared.

The Number One Surfman, A.E. Kristofferson, went over to the Coast Guard Sub Chaser Number 438, which was sheltering in the harbor. The 438, enroute to Grand Marais, Minnesota, to shut down the station there for the season, had just slipped into the harbor before the worst of the storm struck. Surfman Kristofferson asked the 438's captain, G.R. O'Connor for help. Several of the Life-Savers were sick and extra men were needed.

Also, Benjamin Truedell, the legendary Grand Marais Keeper, was on leave and not available.

The H.E. RUNNELS heavily loaded with lumber. Note that her freeing ports are nearly awash.

Lake Superior Marine Museum

O'Connor agreed to provide whatever assistance he could, but he told Kristofferson that he had aboard as a guest, John O. Anderson, the veteran Keeper of the Chicago Station. Could Anderson help? Eagerly Kristofferson accepted the offer.

As Anderson and Kristofferson were walking back to the station, they saw the steamer close ashore on the wrong side of the pier and sounding distress signals. The blizzard was still blowing and visibility was terrible, but she was identified as the H.B. RUNNELS.

The RUNNELS had sheltered in Grand Marais on November 13 from a northwest blow. The next day the weather moderated a bit, so she left to continue her trip. About eight miles out, she was slammed by a renewed gale. Rather than try to push through, she returned to Grand Marais. When her steering gear broke in heavy seas, she went on the offshore bar.

The 182-foot wooden steamer H.E. RUNNELS. The rescue of her crew was one of the most dramatic in the annals of the Coast Guard.

When Anderson and Kristofferson reached the station they discovered that the big power lifeboat was disabled. After the lookout spotted the RUNNELS close in, the station crew had started off in the lifeboat, intending to pick up Kristofferson and additional help at the 438. But enroute the engine stalled. Unable to repair it, the crew had to anchor and wade ashore. For this rescue the lifeboat was out of action. Plan A was out, on to plan B.

Under the direction of Anderson and Kristofferson, the crew, assisted by the Grand Marais Lightkeeper and part of the 438 crew, hauled the beach apparatus to the shore near the west pier opposite the RUNNELS. The steamer was 500-600 yards out, fast on a sandbar.

She continued to blow distress signals.

Turned broadside to the seas, the RUNNELS was being hammered without mercy. Wave after wave smashed into her, each putting another nail into her coffin. In was only a matter of time before she went to pieces and the 17 men aboard would drown.

As made second nature by years of drill, the Station crew professionally set up the beach apparatus, charged the Lyle gun and neatly dropped a messenger line across the steamer's bowsprit. Under the terrible storm conditions, it was quite a feat!

Quickly the RUNNELS' crew hauled away at the light messenger line and brought the block with the whip line aboard. This they secured to the post of the steering wheel in the pilothouse. It was the only object still standing strong enough to serve as an anchor point.

Because the RUNNELS was laying broadside to the seas, a vicious cross sea and current was set up on her leeward side, that side facing the shore. The whip line was caught in the cross current and kept turning the whip block, which fouled. Unable to pull the heavy hawser necessary to support the breeches buoy through the fouled block, any attempt at a breeches buoy rescue was finished. Plan B was out, on to plan C.

The Coast Guardsmen brought both ends of the whip line tightly together into a single double line. The bow line of the light surfboat was run over the doubled line and tied off to the bow shackle. When the shore ends of the whip line were secured to the beach anchor, the whip line could be used as a guide line for the surfboat. No matter what the waves and current did, the surfboat could travel a direct course between the beach and wreck.

With Anderson at the steering oar, the small surfboat headed for the wreck. It was a hellish trip. Several times breakers swept men out of the boat. Each time they struggled back aboard and continued to pull for the RUNNELS. Reaching the wreck, four of the steamer's crew were taken in the surfboat and after great difficulty, safely landed on the beach. The RUNNELS crewmen seemed half dead from exposure.

In total, four trips were made through that terrible boiling surf and all 17 crewmen were saved. The last was perhaps the worst. Instead of the eight rowers normally used, only six men were available. Once the short handed crew reached the wreck, they had the special problem of getting the last two crewmen aboard, the captain, Hugh O'Hagan, and chief engineer, Joseph Hemmeth.

It was intended that the men would slide down the whip line into the surfboat, as did the other crewmen. But both the captain and engineer dropped off short, landing in the water. Each in turn had to be manhandled into the surfboat. In the case of the engineer, who weighed 315 pounds, it was an especially difficult task.

From the official records, only Anderson, Kristofferson and Surfman Russel Martin had the stamina to make all four trips. And that stamina was indeed remarkable. Anderson was washed out of the boat three times, while Kristofferson was swept out at least twice.

On the first trip the boat was manned with station men, volunteers from the 438 and a local fisherman. When they returned to the beach, three of the crewmen were all in. Taken with cramps from the immersion in the cold water and tremendous exertion, they had to be carried away. For the remaining trips, each crew was a different combination of station men, 438 men and local fishermen. One of the fishermen was an ex Life-Saver and knew the drills well. As the crewmen succumbed, volunteers took their places. There were lives to be saved and it was not the place nor the time for the faint hearted.

For the wives of the station crew and fishermen it must have been a difficult time. A local observer reported that there was "no wimpering among the wives of the fishermen who stood on shore and waved encouragement to their menfolk." Captain O'Connor of the 438 also had special praise for the bravery of the fishermen.

The last surfboat reached the shore at 12:40 in the afternoon. Thirty minutes later the RUNNELS broke up. The rescue was just in the nick of time.

The physical abuse suffered by the surfboat crews was terrible. When they were finally finished, their frozen life jackets had to be cut free as well as much of their clothing.

Although Captain O'Connor was the senior Coast Guard Officer on the scene, he left the rescue to the experts, Anderson and Kristofferson. But after the final trip, when he saw how utterly fatigued Kristofferson was, he relieved the trusty Number One Surfman of all responsibility for the beach apparatus and related equipment and for any station duties. He ordered him immediately to bed. This was an extraordinary action on the part of O'Connor since the careful accountability and maintenace of equipment was a hallmark of the Life-Saving crews.

On November 16, Keeper Truedell returned from leave and after learning the details of the desperate work of the previous day, began to put things back to order. Still short handed because of sick Surfman, several local men were hired to clean and recover equipment, repair the broken power lifeboat and generally prepare the station for action, should action be required again.

The RUNNELS rescue demonstrated the indomitable spirit and resourcefulness of the old Life-Saving crews. It had only been four years since the Life-Saving Service was absorbed into the fledging Coast Guard and its strong backbone was still very much evident. When a plan went awry, another was rapidly developed. In spite of the sickness of the crewmen, they toughed it through. When necessary volunteers were used. If the keeper was absent, no problem. The Number One Surfman took charge and accomplished the rescue.

As a tribute to their bravery, the Secretary of the Treasury awarded a gold life-saving medal to each of the men, including Anderson and the four Grand Marais fishermen.

The RUNNELS was a total loss of $60,000. She was no stranger to Lake Superior shipwreck. On November 25, 1897, she stranded during a snow storm on Point Abbaye at the entrance to Huron Bay. She was released with $5,000 in damages. On May 29, 1895, her cargo of coal caught fire when she was on Lake Erie. To extinguish it, she was scuttled in shallow water.

The RUNNELS was built in 1893 at Port Huron, Michigan, by the Jenks Ship Building Company. At the time of her loss, she was owned by O.W. Blodgett of Bay City, Michigan.

REFERENCES:

ANNUAL REPORT, UNITED STATES LIFE-SAVING SERVICE, 1896, op. cit.
Lake Superior Marine Museum Archives. *Duluth, Minnesota.*
Log of the Coast Guard Station No. 296, November 14-18, 1919, op. cit.
SAULT STE. MARIE EVENING NEWS (Michigan). November 16, 21, 22, 1919.
Stuart, William M. *"The Great Lakes Wreck of the H.E. RUNNELS". COAST GUARD MAGAZINE, June 1932.*
Wells, op. cit.

VESSEL:	**MYRON**
LOSS:	**Total**
DATE:	**November 22, 1919**
TYPE:	**Wooden Steamer**
LOCATION:	**Off Whitefish Point**

SYNOPSIS:

One of the worst tragedies of the "shipwreck coast" occurred on November 22, 1919. The victim was the 186-foot, 676-ton wooden steamer MYRON. Before the day was done, the steamer was lost with almost her entire crew.

Earlier that day, the MYRON, towing the 194-foot schooner-barge MIZTEC, departed Munising. Both were loaded with lumber and bound for Buffalo. Aboard the MYRON was a crew of 17, while seven manned the MIZTEC. The MYRON was under the command of Walter R. Neal, a veteran skipper.

Two hours out from Munising the MYRON and MIZTEC were struck by a vicious November gale. Mountainous waves slammed into them as they battled their way eastward. Doubtlessly their seams began to open as a result of working in the seas and water leaked into thier holds. They became less and less able to rise to the cresting seas.

Heavy snow started to fall and the temperature fell rapidly. Thick ice built up on both vessels, changing their center of gravity, making them unstable.

Seeing the trouble the pair was in, Captain McRae of the big 420 foot steel steamer ADRIATIC ran in close aboard and used his bulk to shield the MYRON and MIZTEC from the northwest seas as best he could.

When he had reached Vermilion, Captain Neal decided that in order for the MYRON to have any chance at survival he would have to drop his tow. Maybe then he could just reach safety in the lee of Whitefish Point. The decision was by no means as heartless as it might seem. The MIZTEC would probably be able to weather the blow better if free of the steamer anyway. The MIZTEC dropped the anchors and swung head to the sea. Although battered, she survived to sail again.

Captain Neal continued on for Whitefish, with the ADRIATIC still running interference. The sharp-eyed lookout at the Vermilion Coast Guard Station sighted the strange struggle and alerted the crew. There was work to be done!

174

The lumber hooker MYRON. On November 27, 1919, she foundered off Whitefish Point with the loss of all hands except one.

Despite the wild surf, the Vermilion crew launched their motor lifeboat and headed out for the MYRON. They doubted she would make the Point. If the steamer's crew was to live, the Coast Guard would be badly needed. Through crashing seas the small motor lifeboat chased the MYRON in a desperate race for life. But the Coast Guardsmen lost the race.

About a mile and a half northwest of Whitefish Point the MYRON's boiler fires flooded and without power, she slipped into the deadly trough. The crew ran for her two lifeboats. Working speedily they managed to launch both just minutes before she sank. A tremendous field of wreckage from the steamer as well as her lumber cargo surrounded both boats. The field was so thick that the crewmen couldn't force their way out. They were trapped within.

In the gathering darkness, Captain McRae tried to reach the survivors in the ADRIATIC, but the big steamer touched bottom twice. Afraid for his vessel, he refused to try again.

Another vessel was also watching the drama. When Captain Lawrence of the big 520-foot steel steamer H.P. LAWRENCE saw the ADRIATIC fail, he gave it a try. He forced his steamer through the seething wreckage field close enough to be able to actually throw lines to the MYRON crewmen. But the crewmen were so numbed by the freezing temperatures that they couldn't grasp them with their frozen hands! Also fearing for the safety of his vessel in the dangerous shallow water, Captain Lawrence ran for open water.

Meanwhile the Vermilion Coast Guard crew had reached the site, but the churning mass of spars, lines, lumber and all manner of floating debris was too much. Sadly the Coast Guardsmen realized they could not possibly force their way through it to reach the two boat loads of half dead survivors.

Eventually the frozen bodies of the crew were recovered. All wore life jackets and were covered with ice. Some were frozen into grotesqsue shapes. Taken to a Soo funeral home, they actually had to be thawed out next to a roaring fire. Others were discovered frozen into shore ice and had to be chopped free.

The only survivor from the MYRON was Captain Neal. He was in the pilothouse when the steamer sank. When she went under, the wooden pilothouse popped off. Neal climbed through the window and on to the rock. There he held on for nearly a full day. Off Parisienne Island he was picked up by the steamer W.C. FRANZ. She was on the lookout for bodies from the wreck but hardly expected to find Neal floating along on the pilothouse! Neal's hands were so swelled from the cold, that two finger rings were not visible. He recovered from his ordeal to sail again.

Captain Neal was extremely upset at the failure of the ADRIATIC and H.P. MCINTOSH to rescue his crew. He bitterly charged criminal behavior.

At a special hearing by the Steamboat Inspection Service, Neal stated that "I was clinging to the roof of the pilothouse when the MCINTOSH hailed me shortly after the MYRON went down from under me. The MCINTOSH drew alongside me, not more than 16 feet away. Although it was dusk, the ship was so close that I had no difficulty in making out her name. I talked to the captain and expected that he would put out a yawl and pick me up. He did not do so, nor attempt in any way to help me. 'I will have a boat sent for you,' the captain of the MCINTOSH called. And he drew away. I have never seen him since, nor do I ever want to see him, by the great hokey pokey."

The Steamboat Inspection Service agreed with Captain Neal and the licenses of both masters were revoked for life for "failure to render aid and assistance." The marine community felt the penalty was far too extreme, considering the effort the men made. There is no record whether an appeal later restored their licenses or lessened the penalty.

The MIZTEC came through the storm without serious damage. The tug IOWA eventually towed her to the Soo. She had lost most of her deck cargo and rudder. She would sail for two more years.

The MYRON was built in 1888 at Grand Haven, Michigan. Originally the MARK HOPKINS, she was renamed MYRON in 1902. With a single cargo hold amidships, she could carry 950 tons or 7000,000 board feet of lumber. Technically she was a "lumber hooker," one of a class built especially for the lumber trade. She was a loss of $45,000.

The wreck of the MYRON was discovered in 1972 by John Steele and Tom Farnquist. It rests shattered by surf and ice on a sand bottom in 50-feet. Wrecks in such shallow water are not treated kindly. The boiler, engine and machinery is still present and the wreck is becoming an increasingly popular diving target. Her builder's plate was recovered in 1979 by Great Lakes Historical Society divers which positively identified the wreck.

177

REFERENCES:

EVENING NEWS (Sault Ste. Marie, Michigan). Novem-
ber 24, 25, 26, 28, 29, December 1, 2, 3, 4, 5, 1919.
Great Lakes Shipwreck Historical Society Archives.
GREAT LAKES SHIPWRECK QUARTERLY, Volume 2,
Number 2, op. cit.
Johnson, Ken. "Strange Story of the Steamer MYRON".
DIVER, September 1984.
LeLieve, Roger. "Shipwreck Victims Washed Ashore
to Lonely Graves". UPBEAT, February 4, 1979.
MARQUETTE MINING JOURNAL. November 24, 25, 26
December 2, 3, 4, 1919.
Runge Collection. Milwaukee Public Library.
Wells, op. cit.

VESSEL:	**SUPERIOR CITY**
LOSS:	**Total**
DATE:	**August 20, 1920**
TYPE:	**Steel Steamer**
LOCATION:	**Whitefish Bay**

SYNOPSIS:

About 9:15 p.m. on August 20, 1920, approximately five miles southeast of Whitefish Point, two vessels, the downbound 429-foot, 4,795-ton SUPERIOR CITY and upbound 580-foot WILLIS L. KING came together with a fearful crash. The KING's bow tore deeply into the port side of the SUPERIOR CITY, just aft of the midships marks. It was clear to all that the heavily laden SUPERIOR CITY was doomed.

The crew of the SUPERIOR CITY rushed desperately to leave their sinking steamer. But most were already too late! There wasn't even enough time to launch the lifeboats. Water flooded into the boiler room

The 429-foot SUPERIOR CITY. After the 580-foot
WILLIS L. KING collided with her in Whitefish Bay,
she sank with the loss of 29 men.

Three of the crew, including the captain, were
recovered by the KING. One was holding on to a life
preserver, another hanging to a capsized lifeboat, while
the third was treading water. Luckily the lake was
calm. The fourth survivor was plucked off a floating
wooden hatch cover by the steamer J.J. TURNER.

The collision was the result of confusion between

the two vessels as to whether the passing was to be port to port or starboard to starboard. At the last minute the SUPERIOR CITY turned across the KING's bow.

Owned by the Pittsburg Steamship Company, the SUPERIOR CITY was a loss of $650,000. The KING's bow needed $30,000 for repairs. The SUPERIOR CITY was built in 1898 by the Lorain yard of the Cleveland Shipbuilding Company. It was the first vessel launched at the new shipyard.

The wreck of the SUPERIOR CITY was initially discovered in 1972 by Great Lakes diver John Steele. Resting in 265 feet of water, she is nearly intact. Rediscovered in 1980 by Tom Farnquist and Gary Shumbarger of the Great Lakes Shipwreck Historical Society, she has been extensively filmed by the group.

REFERENCES:

CLEVELAND PLAIN DEALER. August 22, 23, 1920.
Correspondence, Steamboat Inspection Service, reference the SUPERIOR CITY-WILLIS L. KING Collision. National Archives and Records Service, Washington, D.C.
GREAT LAKES SHIPWRECK QUARTERLY, Volume 2, Number 4, 1983, op. cit.
Lake Superior Marine Museum Archives. Duluth, Minnesota.
LiLieve, Roger. "Two Different Stories Were Told". PEOPLE AND PLACES, March 3, 1975.
LORAIN TIMES (Lorain Ohio). April 13, 1898.
Report of Casualty, U.S. Coast Guard, SUPERIOR CITY. National Archives and Records Service. Washington, D.C.
SAULT STE. MARIE EVENING NEWS. August 21, 23, 24, 25, 26, 28, 1920.
Sanderson, PICTORIAL MARINE HISTORY, op. cit.
Wells, op. cit.
Wright, FRESHWATER WHALES, op. cit.

VESSEL:	**MIZTEC**
LOSS:	Total
DATE:	May 14, 1921
TYPE:	Schooner-Barge
LOCATION:	Vermilion Point

SYNOPSIS:

Traditionally a spring gale never packed the power of a fall blow, but sometimes they did come close. The May 14, 1921 loss of the 194-foot, 777-ton schooner-barge MIZTEC is a case in point.

The MIZTEC, together with the schooner-barge PESHTIGO, was in tow of the 202-foot wooden steamer ZILLAH. The MIZTEC and ZILLAH carried salt cargos for Duluth, while the PESHTIGO was empty and due to be dropped off at Munising.

The small fleet was making reasonable progress in stormy weather until about ten miles west of Whitefish Point. There the full fury of a spring gale slammed into them. Deciding not to try to punch through, the captain of the ZILLAH elected to return to the lee of Whitefish Point. However, the strain of the turn parted the tow lines and the MIZTEC and PESHTIGO were left to their own devices. Unburdened by the two tows, the ZILLAH was able to work her way to safety behind the Point.

After setting a short set of sails, the PESHTIGO tried to reach the Point too. But the screaming north wind soon shredded her canvas. Near Vermilion Point she dropped her anchors to try to ride out the gale. The wind and waves were so strong that even with both hooks down, she was still dragging toward the beach. If she struck the offshore bar, or blew ashore, the deadly breakers would smash her to pieces. The Vermilion Coast Guard sighted the troubled vessel and attempted to reach her but failed. The crashing seas destroyed both of their surfboats! Helplessly, they watched what they thought would be the destruction of the PESHTIGO. As if by a miracle, her anchors caught, holding her about a quarter mile offshore. Vessel and crew survived.

The MIZTEC was not so lucky. She foundered an estimated three miles offshore, taking all seven hands down with her. The lake had claimed another victim.

The schooner-barge MIZTEC. On May 14, 1921, she foundered with all hands off Vermilion Point.

The Coast Guard Cutter COOK later located a spar from the MIZTEC sticking out of the shallow water west of Whitefish Point. The Cook buoyed it as a navigation hazard but a later storm blew it off. When the COOK returned to replace the buoy, the wreck couldn't be relocated. At the time the theory was advanced that the salt cargo had dissolved, thus allowing the wreck to "sail along the bottom into deeper water."

In a strange coincidence, the MIZTEC sank very close to the location where the old two steamer MYRON sank two years before. The MIZTEC had survived that blow. The coincidences didn't end here. The only survivor of the MYRON was her master, Walter R. Neal. He was working as the mate of the ZILLAH when the MIZTEC foundered.

Owned by O.W. Blodgett, the MIZTEC was a loss of $10,000. The MIZTEC was built in 1890 at Marine City by J.H. Jenken for the Marine City Transit Company. There were four vessels in the fleet; two steamers, the AZTEC and TOLTEC and two schooner-barges, the ZAPOTEC and MIZTEC. The fleet normally worked the ore and lumber trade.

The wreck of the MIZTEC is in 45 to 50-feet of water. What's left is broken and scattered but visibility is usually excellent. One anchor is still present as is the chain and other items of gear. The wreck was discovered by the Oddessey Foundation in 1983.

REFERENCES:

Gammage, Mark. "Discovery of the Schooner MIZTEC." GREAT LAKES SHIPWRECK QUARTERLY, Fall 1984.
Lake Superior Marine Museum Archives. Duluth, Minnesota.
MARQUETTE MINING JOURNAL. May 16, 17, 1921.
Runge Collection, Milwaukee Public Library.
Wolff, SHIPWRECKS OF LAKE SUPERIOR, op. cit.

VESSEL:	**ARBUTUS**
LOSS:	**Total**
DATE:	**November 24, 1921**
TYPE:	**Tug**
LOCATION:	**Off Grand Marais**

SYNOPSIS:

Heavy weather on November 24, 1921, caused the loss of the 34-ton tug ARBUTUS about ten miles northeast of Grand Marais. The ARBUTUS had earlier been used as a rum runner, sailing between the Canadian shore and the Keweenaw. Prohibition may have been the law of the land, but somewhere else, not in the U.P.! Besides, without a doubt the cargo of the ARBUTUS was intended for medicinal use only.

The ARBUTUS was finally caught through the ineptitude of her crew. It seems after slipping into Copper Harbor, on the west side of the Keweenaw, her crew began sampling the cargo. They whooped up such a party that the lighthouse keeper, to his eternal shame, alerted Federal agents.

The "Feds" laid her up in Marquette to await final disposition. Eventually she was released to the Canadian bank that held a lien on her. The bank in turn sold her to a Captain F.E. Fader of Fort William. While sailing to the Soo, she was lost.

REFERENCES:

Winkleman, SHIPPING CASUALTIES, op. cit.
Wolff, Dr. Julius F. Jr. "Canadian Shipwrecks on Lake Superior". INLAND SEAS, Winter 1978.

VESSEL:	**LAMBTON**
LOSS:	**Total**
DATE:	**April 19, 1922**
TYPE:	**Lighthouse Tender**
LOCATION:	**Unknown**

SYNOPSIS:

The third vessel that "went missing" in the Whitefish area was the lighthouse tender LAMBTON. She disappeared on April 19, 1922.

The LAMBTON was built in the Canadian Government Shipyard at Sorel in 1909. At 108-feet overall, 25-feet in beam and 13-feet in depth, she was a small vessel to face Superior's gales, but over the years she had proven herself to be well found and seaworthy. Technically she was known as a "lighthouse supply and buoy vessel" and performed this service regularly, being responsible for the area from Quebec north to the Upper Lakes.

The tug W.R. GRAY lead the search for the missing LAMBTON. Shown here she is fully decked out to celebrate her 1920 arrival in the Soo.

Hamilton Collection

The LAMBTON left the Canadian Soo Thursday April 18, 1922. She was headed upbound to place the lights at Parisienne, Caribou and Michipicoten Islands into operation. Aboard were 22 men, including crew and keepers.

At the time, strong northwest gales were sweeping the lake and snow squalls were reported in some

185

locations. The powerful winds had also packed drifting ice into Whitefish Bay, and area that had previously been free of ice.

The steamer MIDLAND PRINCE. She lost track of the smaller LAMBTON in the middle of the gale.

Hamilton Collection

At 8:30 p.m., April 19, the Soo was struck by a severe windstorm out of the northwest. Since the LAMBTON was known to be out on the lake, there was concern for her safety. Radio messages were sent to all vessels asking if any knew if the LAMBTON was safe.

On April 23 the downbound Canadian steamer VALCARTIER reported that on the 20th, "about 25 miles southeast of Michipicoten Island and 15 miles east of Caribou, saw what looked like a top of a small pilothouse painted white, trimmed with bright red," and some additional wreckage. The wheelsman on the VALCARTIER had sailed the year before on the

186

LAMBTON and he was sure it was her pilothouse.

An extensive search failed to find any additional wreckage. The small LAMBTON was gone. Exactly why she was lost was never determined. One theory held it was as the result of damage suffered to her steering gear while helping free an icebound steamer on Whitefish Bay on the 18th. Later, stressed by the storm, her damaged steering gear failed and the LAMBTON foundered.

While attempting to free the big steel steamer GLEN-FINNAN from an ice jam in Whitefish Bay, the LAMBTON collided with her port quarter. Although no damage was apparent at the time, the LAMBTON's steering gear later failed. Was there a connection?

Hamilton Collection

Like the ADELLA SHORES and D.M. CLEMSON the wreck of the LAMBTON has never been located. She still sails as part of the "went missing fleet".

Note: A more complete examination of the LAMBTON loss can be found in *Went Missing*, Avery Color Studios, Au Train, Michigan 49806.

Small when compared to the larger SIMCOE, the
Canadian Government Vessel LAMBTON was still
seaworthy enough to perform her job as a lighthouse
tender, at least until that fateful day in April 1922.

Ministry of Transport

REFERENCES:

*Appleton, Thomas E. UNQUE AD MARE, A HISTORY
OF THE CANADIAN COAST AND MARINE SERVICES.
(Ottawa: Department of Transportation, 1968).
Canadian Public Archives, Ottawa.
DAILY MINING JOURNAL (Marquette Mining Journal).
April 20, 25, 26, 1922.
TORONTO GLOBE. April 20, 25, 26, 1922.*

VESSEL:	HURONTON
LOSS:	Total
DATE:	October 11, 1922
TYPE:	Steel Steamer
LOCATION:	Off Whitefish Point

SYNOPSIS:

On October 11, 1923, fog again caused grief for a vessel. This time it was the 238-foot, 1,945-ton Canadian steel steamer HURONTON. Upbound, she was struck fatally by the 416-foot, 4,720-ton American freighter CETUS. The crash occurred about 30 miles northwest of Whitefish Point.

The Canadian steamer HURONTON was another victim of collision, sinking on October 11, 1922, after being struck by the steamer CETUS.

To allow enough time for the HURONTON's crew to escape, the captain of the CETUS kept his bow plugged into the Canadian until all of the crew were accounted for. Then he backed out and the HURON-TON quickly sank.

Owned by the Mathews Steamship Company, she was a loss of $100,000. Built as a package freight canaller in 1898 at Lorain, Ohio, by the Cleveland Shipbuilding Company for the Soo Line Railroad, she was originally named the HURON. In 1916, as the tremendous demand for shipping due to World War I, she went salt water. She returned to the lakes in 1919.

REFERENCES:

ANNUAL REPORT OF THE LAKE CARRIER's ASSOCIATION, 1931.
DETROIT MARINE HISTORIAN, October 1983, op. cit.
Mills, *CANADIAN COASTAL,* op. cit.
Wells, op. cit.
Winkleman, *SHIPPING CASUALTIES,* op. cit.

VESSEL:	J.L. CRANE
LOSS:	Total
DATE:	November 5, 1925
TYPE:	Wooden Barge
LOCATION:	Crisp Point

SYNOPSIS:

The gales of November came calling in deadly earnest on November 5, 1925. On that date the 210-foot wooden steamer HERMAN H. HETTLER was towing the 187-foot, 548-ton wooden barge J.L. CRANE. Both were downbound with pulp wood. The weather was truly terrible, with a screaming 80 mile per hour northwest wind, driving snow and hull wrenching waves. But the HETTLER and CRANE seemed to be toughing it out until about 10:30 p.m. Suddenly the running lights of the CRANE blinked out. At the same instant, the towing stern post of the HETTLER ripped out like it was made of mere balsa wood! The CRANE had foundered! She suddenly dove for the bottom and her dead weight resulted in the hawser snapping out the steamer's stern post.

Unable to come about and look for any of the CRANE's crew because of the storm, the HETTLER continued to the lee of Whitefish Point. When she finally dropped her anchors behind the Point's safety, she was leaking badly. The HETTLER had survived, only to be lost on November 23, 1926, in Munising's east channel.

The entire crew of the CRANE, five men and one woman cook, went down with her. The wreck was eventually discovered by the Coast Guard approximately a mile off the Crisp Point Station in 25 feet of water. Like the MIZTEC, the CRANE was owned by O.W. Blogett of Bay City. She was the only shipwreck in the Upper Lakes that year.

REFERENCES:

ANNUAL REPORT OF THE LAKE CARRIER's ASSOCIATION, 1925, op. cit.
DULUTH NEWS-TRIBUNE. November 7, 8, 27, 1925.
Wells, op. cit.

VESSEL:	ZILLAH
LOSS:	Total
DATE:	August 29, 1926
TYPE:	Wooden Steamer
LOCATION:	Whitefish Bay

SYNOPSIS:

Although the traditional time for storm losses is the fall, on occasion a summer gale can strike with fatal consequences. On August 29, 1926, the old wooden steamer ZILLAH was caught by such a gale.

The lumber hooker ZILLAH was another victim of a Whitefish gale. Note the "string" of schooner-barges she is towing.

Marine Historical Collection,
Milwaukee Public Library

Built in 1890 at West Bay City, by the F.W. Wheeler Company, she was one of the older wooden steamers still working. Originally launched as the EDWARD SMITH, she was renamed in 1901. With a length of 202 feet and 1,100 tons, she had a capacity of 800,000 board feet of lumber. But it wasn't lumber she carried into the August blow, but a heavy load of limestone.

The ZILLAH's situation, reduced to a near sinking condition by the storm, was observed by the Whitefish Point Coast Guard lookout, as well as the big steel steamers KENTOSA and WILLIAM B. SCHILLER. When it became apparent that she was going down, all rushed to her aid.

The Coast Guard reached her first. The steamers stood off as the nimble Coast Guard motor lifeboat dashed in and removed all the crew. Approximately four miles south of Whitefish Point, the ZILLAH foundered. She was a loss of $50,000.

The ZILLAH was discovered in 1975 in 252-feet of water by Kent Bellrichard.

REFERENCES:

ANNUAL REPORT OF THE LAKE CARRIER's ASSOCIATION, 1926, op. cit.
Great Lakes Shipwreck Historical Society Archives.
MARQUETTE MINING JOURNAL. August 30, 1926.
Runge Collection. Milwaukee Public Library.
Wells, op. cit.

VESSEL:	**LAMBTON**
LOSS:	**Recovered**
DATE:	**December 8, 1927**
TYPE:	**Steel Steamer**
LOCATION:	**Parisienne Island**

SYNOPSIS:

During December 7-8, 1927, a terrific storm struck Lake Superior. A true hell-bender, four modern steel freighters were wrecked; the 250-foot KAMLOOPS disappeared with all hands near Isle Royale, the 356-foot ALTADOC was cast ashore on Keweenaw Point, the 375-foot E.W. OGLEBAY swept on to Shot Point just east of Marquette and the 252-foot LAMBTON was blown on a reef off Parisienne Island, Whitefish Bay.

The LAMBTON departed Fort William downbound with grain on Tuesday, December 6. The next afternoon she ran into a blinding snowstorm and roaring north gale. Sub-zero temperatures had frozen spray and the LAMBTON was a thick mass of ice. Heavily burdened by the ice, in some places two feet thick, the crew wondered just how long the steamer could continue to stay afloat.

Unable to fix her position, she proceeded as carefully as possible, but 4 p.m. Thursday, December 8, she struck a shoal off Parisienne Island with a tremendous jolt. Impaled on the rocks, she waited to die. Remembering the ice, the chief engineer later stated "I wouldn't have given 25 cents for our chances of coming through alive even before the crash."

With her bottom ripped open, the water quickly flooded into the engine room extinguishing her boiler fires. Now the crew was without heat except for the small fire kept burning in the galley stove. Soon all of the below deck compartments flooded and the crew was forced to remain on the open decks.

Immediately after striking, an attempt to lower one of the lifeboats was made, but just as it reached the water, a huge wave struck the LAMBTON and ripped it free of the davits. In a boil of water it was gone, snapping the inch thick lines as if they were twine. The second lifeboat was damaged in the attempt to launch it, so it was hauled back aboard.

For a short period on Thursday night, Whitefish Point Light was visible. To signal distress, the crew burned huge flares hastily made from black paint and

194

oakum on the roof of the pilothouse. The flares went unseen.

About noon on Friday, two crewmen made a desperate and ill-fated attempt to reach shore. They donned patent life suits, similar to the suit a hard hat diver would use. The suits were intended to keep the wearer warm and dry, thus allowing him to survive frigid water. The pair lashed themselves together with a line, jumped overboard and headed for shore. They quickly disappeared in the boiling lake.

On Saturday the storm moderated, and shortly past noon the second lifeboat was launched after hasty repairs. The LAMBTON was giving signs of breaking up completely and it was prudent to leave her as rapidly as possible. Loaded down with the 18 remaining crewmen, the small boat struck out for the Canadian mainland.

The steamer LAMBTON in the Portage Canal after being salvaged from Parisienne Island. She had wrecked there the year before.

K.E. Thro

195

It was a dangerous trip. Water entered as quickly as three men could bail it out, but they persevered About dark, they came ashore near Goulais Point on the Canadian coast. After hiking 15 miles around the point, the frozen, bedraggled survivors reached an abandoned cabin where they promptly started a much welcome fire. During the tramp along the cold and deserted beach, they discovered the lifeboat lost the previous day, complete with the provisions they had carefully secured aboard. The survivors considered it a miracle the small boat hadn't been destroyed by the waves or smashed to pieces on the beach. Some of the food was cooked right next to the boat by the heat of a hastily built bonfire. The rest was carried along, eventually to be eaten in the deserted cabin.

The next day the survivors continued their march, arriving at the Indian fishing village of Goulais Mission the next day. There they were cared for and word sent to the Soo of their safety.

The crew came through the wreck in remarkably good shape, their worst injuries being frostbite and exposure. All praised their captain, Andrew Livingstone, for keeping the crew together (except for the two who jumped overboard) and leading them out of what could have been a true disaster. Only 34 years old, Livingstone was one of the youngest masters on the lakes.

Shipwreck was not a new experience for some of the crew. The chief engineer had been wrecked three times before and the second engineer twice, one being the 1924 wreck of the GLENLYON at Isle Royale.

Although it wasn't apparent to the LAMBTON crew, a passing vessel did sight the wreck and relayed the information to the Coast Guard at Whitefish Point. But when the Coast Guard reached the LAMBTON, they discovered her abandoned. The crew had already left in the lifeboat.

The LAMBTON was hauled off the next spring by the famous wrecker Tom Reid. Too far gone to be used as a steamer, her engines were removed and she was reduced to a barge.

196

The 1,866-ton LAMBTON was built in 1921 at Port Arthur as the GLENAFTON. Owned by the Mathews Steamship Company of Toronto, she was a loss of $150,000.

REFERENCES:

ANNUAL REPORT OF THE LAKE CARRIER's ASSOCIATION, 1927, op. cit.
DAILY MINING GAZETTE (Houghton, Michigan). December 13, 1927.
FORT WILLIAM DAILY TIMES-JOURNAL. December 12, 13, 1927.
Memorandum, Public Archives of Canada to Author, February 10, 1975.

VESSEL:	**LYDIA**
LOSS:	**Total**
DATE:	**November 25, 1932**
TYPE:	**Fish Tug**
LOCATION:	**Off Grand Marais**

SNYOPSIS:

On November 25, 1932, three fish tugs were working the grounds in the northeast corner of the lake when a roaring northwest gale struck. Two of the tugs, the ISABELLA and ADDISON, safely sheltered behind Caribou and Michipicoten Islands. The third, the 47-foot, 54-ton LYDIA, under Captain Larson of Racine, Wisconsin, ran for Grand Marais.

At 5:55 p.m. the watchman in the Grand Marais Coast Guard Station lookout tower sighted a fish tug heading for the harbor. Called by the lookout, the

Station Officer in Charge, Chief Bosun Mate A.C. Gross, climbed the tower to watch.

The small vessel seemed to be proceeding through the heavy seas fine and was having no special trouble. At 6:05 p.m. as she was entering the channel, a large breaker caught the tug on her starboard after quarter and turned her completely over. Her lights went out when she rolled and in the gathering darkness nothing more was seen of her.

Gross immediately sounded the station alarm and launched his motor lifeboat. As the Coast Guard headed for the channel, the intensity of the gale increased and snow squalls lashed the area. Using the boat search light and hand flash lights, they searched the channel into the harbor as well as the point where the tug went under. Battling the huge waves made their work nearly impossible, but still they tried. They found nothing.

Since they discovered nothing in the channel, Gross ran back into the harbor and moored his boat. On foot the Coast Guardsmen searched the shore. They found much wreckage, including parts of her deckhouse and many fish boxes, but no clues to the five men aboard. In fact, no bodies were immediately found, in spite of the Coast Guards diligent search to include later dragging the channel.

The best guess the Coast Guard made was that the bodies were tangled in fish nets and trapped beneath the tug's hull. Later, when the boiler and hull were located about 900 feet from shore and 400 feet east of the pier, Gross decided they would investigate. Borrowing a hard hat diving suit and air pump from Coast Guard Headquarters at the Soo, and an experienced diver, Boatswain Paul Liedtke, from the Deer Park Station, the Grand Marais crew arranged to search the hull. The diver found nothing. On December 4 and 5, two bodies were finally found on the beach west of Deer Park. They were reportedly the only ones ever recovered.

REFERENCES:

GRAND MARAIS PILOT *(Grand Marais, Michigan).*
December 3, 1975.
Log of the Grand Marais Coast Guard Station, November
25 - December 10, 1932, op. cit.
PORTAGE LAKE MINING GAZETTE *(Houghton,*
Michigan). November 26, 27, 1932.

VESSEL:	**EDDIE S.**
LOSS:	**Total**
DATE:	**May 22, 1945**
TYPE:	**Fish Tug**
LOCATION:	**Grand Marais**

SYNOPSIS:

A sudden north squall on May 22, 1945, caused the
loss of the 45-foot fish tug EDDIE S. The tug was
lost at the identical spot the LYDIA sank. Of the three
men aboard, two were drown. Quick action by the
Coast Guard saved the third. Fishing always a hard
and difficult business, one in which the fishermen often
paid with the lives.

REFERENCES:

GRAND MARAIS PILOT (Grand Marais, Michigan).
December 3, 1975.
MARQUETTE MINING JOURNAL. May 23, 1945.

VESSEL:	ROCKAWAY
LOSS:	Total
DATE:	July 3, 1945
TYPE:	Fish Tug
LOCATION:	Grand Marais

SYNOPSIS:

On July 3, 1945, another fish tug sank about a mile northeast of Grand Marais. The tug ROCKAWAY, with four men aboard, apparently sank as the result of a sudden southwest squall. All aboard were killed. The squall was the most logical answer, some of the wreckage indicated there had been an explosion aboard.

REFERENCES:

MARQUETTE MINING JOURNAL. July 6, 1945.

VESSEL:	VERNON
LOSS:	Total
DATE:	August 5, 1950
TYPE:	Fish Tug
LOCATION:	Grand Marais

SYNOPSIS:

On August 5, 1950, the 13-ton fish tug VERNON was rammed in the fog and sunk by the steamer HARVEY COLBY. The collision occurred 27 miles northeast of Grand Marais. All aboard the VERNON were rescued.

REFERENCES:

Carter, James L. *VOYAGEUR's HARBOR.* *(Grand Marais, Michigan: Pilot Press, 1971).*

VESSEL: **EDMUND FITZGERALD**
LOSS: **Total**
DATE: **November 10, 1975**
TYPE: **Steel Freighter**
LOCATION: **Off Whitefish Point**

SYNOPSIS:

The greatest tragedy of modern Great Lakes history was the November 10, 1975 loss of the 729-foot ore carrier EDMUND FITZGERALD with all 29 men. To this day, the exact cause of the loss is still in dispute. Some thought the hatch covers leaked; some that she hit an uncharted shoal and staggered off to sink in deep water; others believed she just snapped in two on the surface due to hull stress. But one fact is beyond question. The big carrier, once the "pride of the line," rests on the bottom of Lake Superior.

The story starts at 2:15 p.m., November 9, when the FITZGERALD left the ore dock in Superior, Wisconsin. She had just finished loading 27,300 tons of taconite pellets and was downbound for Detroit. About two hours later she met the ARTHUR M ANDERSON off Two Harbors, Minnesota. The ANDERSON fell in about ten miles behind the FITZGERALD and both vessels continued downbound. Ahead, unknown to the two, was the maw of a tremendous Lake Superior Norther'.

By 7 p.m., both vessels had received gale warnings. At 3 a.m., November 10, those warnings were upgraded to storm warnings and both vessels chose to follow the north shore of Lake Superior for protection. The winds were blowing at 52 knots from the northeast and the waves were running at 12 feet. It would be a rough run, but nothing that a big freighter couldn't bull it's way through.

About 10 a.m., both vessels made a series of course changes designed to bring them into the Soo. The winds had decreased to 30 knots but the seas were still 12 feet. by 1:45 p.m., the winds had dropped to 5 knots, but it was only a lull. An hour later the wind was up to 42 knots and shifted from the northeast to northwest.

In the blowing snow and scud, the ANDERSON lost visual sight of the FITZGERALD. The ANDERSON's decks were awash with 16 foot waves.

Both vessels were approaching Caribou Island and Caribou Shoal. The ANDERSON altered course to be well clear, but the FITZGERALD didn't and in the ANDERSON's captain's words "was closer than I would have wanted to be." The observation of the ANDERSON regarding the FITZGERALD's actions proved important. She was the nearest to a witness there would be.

At 3:30 p.m., the FITZGERALD reported by radio to the ANDERSON, "that she "had a fence rail down, two vents damaged and a list," and her pumps were going. The FITZGERALD gave no report as to what had caused the damage. The seas were now cresting at 18 feet. Both the FITZGERALD and ANDERSON continued to plow on for the Soo.

At approximately 4 p.m., the FITZGERALD spoke to an upbound salt water vessel, the AVAFORS and mentioned he had a "bad list, lost both radars and was taking heavy seas over his decks in one of the worst seas he had ever been in."

Two hours later pilothouse crew of the ANDERSON remembered encountering 25 foot waves and at the request of the FITZGERALD, began tracking her on radar. In other words, the FITZGERALD, already damaged, was now in even worse sea conditions. Accurate wind measures were difficult to determine on the open lake, but at this time the Soo Locks closed with reported 90 m.p.h. gusts!

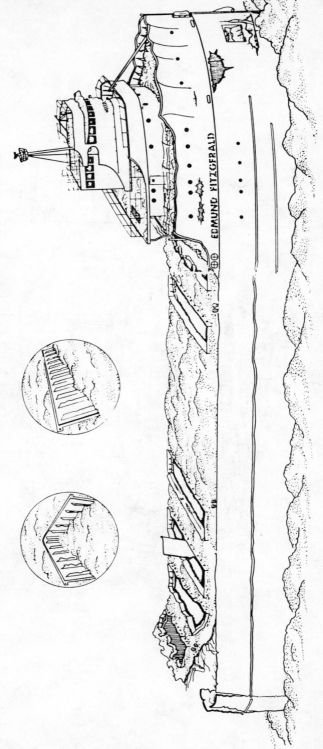

The tremendous damage sustained by the FITZGERALD is evident in these two computer generated mosaics produced by the photographs taken by the CURV III.

U.S. Coast Guard

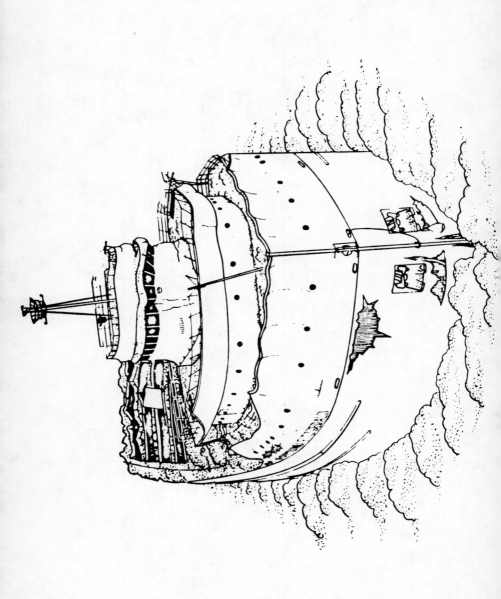

Approximately 17 miles northwest of Whitefish Point and shelter, the FITZGERALD made her last contact with the ANDERSON. The radio call was made at 7:10 p.m. and the pilothouse crew reported that "they were holding their own". Minutes later the big FITZGERALD disappeared from the ANDERSON's radar screen. Whatever happened was so quick that there wasn't even time for a man to pick up a microphone and yell! She was there and then she was gone!

Immediately the ANDERSON started to contact all other vessels in the area, but none had any idea where the FITZGERALD was. At 8:25 p.m. the ANDERSON notified the Coast Guard concerning the missing freighter. The Coast Guard Rescue and Coordination Center at Cleveland responded with a massive search effort. Fixed wing aircraft, helicopters and boats all searched for the FITZGERALD, without luck.

In the following three days surprisingly little wreckage was located. Both lifeboats, or the pieces thereof, were discovered off Coppermine Point, Ontario, as were both liferafts. All were empty and furnished no clues. Bits and pieces of 21 life jackets were also found, as was a light and other miscellaneous wreckage. Little enough for a 729-foot ore carrier.

The hull of the FITZGERALD was located on November 14 by Navy anti-submarine aircraft. It was just where the big freighter had disappeared from the ANDERSON's radar. Later detailed sonar searches confirmed the location and depth, 556 feet.

In May of 1976, the Coast Guard performed an extensive survey of the wreckage using a CURV III (Cable Controlled Underwater Recovery Vehicle), a special remote controlled device. The CURV located two major sections of wreckage, a 253-foot section of the forward portion of the vessel sitting upright and a 276-foot section of the stern resting upside down. The missing 200-foot of her midships was reduced to crushed and shattered hull plates. It was buried in the mud between the fore and aft sections.

The No. 2 lifeboat of the FITZGERALD. Recovered off
Coppermine Point, it was badly damaged when it broke
free from the davits.

U.S. Coast Guard

Since the CURV was equipped with both still
and TV cameras and underwater lights, it was able to
fully document the wreckage. In 12 dives the CURV
recorded 43,255 feet of video tape and 895 still photos.

After a very careful investigation, including a
detailed analysis of the CURV photography, the Coast
Guard reached several conclusions. The technical
aspects of the loss are very complicated. Presented
here are only the most salient features. Since there
were no survivors and no witnesses, the Coast Guard
thought "the proximate cause of the loss of the S.S.
EDMUND FITZGERALD cannot be determined." But
they did think the most probable "cause of the sinking
of the S.S. EDMUND FITZGERALD was the loss of

buoyancy and stability which resulted from massive flooding of the cargo hold." The flooding took place through "ineffective hatch closures as boarding seas rolled along the spar deck." Built as a straight decker, the FITZGERALD had 21 separate cargo hatches. The Coast Guard felt the flooding began early on November 10 and continued throughout the storm until the FITZGERALD gradually lost freeboard and plunged.

The Coast Guard determined that the FITZGERALD didn't strike Caribou Shoal, as seemed possible by the ANDERSON's observation. The investigators were unable to determine what caused her reported topside damage.

The 729-foot EDMUND FITZGERALD . On November 10, 1975, she sank with all 29 hands in the midst of a terrific Lake Superior storm.

Author's Collection

As required by law, the National Transportation Safety Board reviewed the Coast Guard report and disagreed! The NTSB concluded that "the probable cause........was the sudden massive flooding of the cargo hold due to the *collapse of one or more hatch covers.* Before the hatch covers collapsed, flooding into the ballast tanks and tunnel through topside damage and flooding into the cargo hold through nonweathertight hatch covers caused a reduction of freeboard and a list. The hydrostatic and hydrodynamic forces imposed on the hatch covers by heavy boarding seas at this reduced freeboard and with the list, caused the hatch covers to collapse."

But although officialdom may argue the cause, the results are without dispute; the 729-foot EDMUND FITZGERALD lay at the bottom of Lake Superior with all 29 hands. Not a single body was ever recovered. It has long been said that Lake Superior keeps her dead. In the case of the FITZGERALD it's all too true.

The FITZGERALD was built in 1958 by the Great Lakes Engineering Works in River Rouge, Michigan. She cost 8.4 million dollars to build, but inflation made her an estimated loss of 20 million. Owned by the Northwestern Mutual Life Insurance Company, she was operated by the Columbia Transportation Division of Oglebay Norton. She and her sister ship, the ARTHUR B. HOMER, were the largest vessels on the Great Lakes until 1971. During her career she set numerous cargo records. In every respect, she was the "Pride of the Line."

No human diver has ever explored the wreck. Modern diving technology using mixed gases allows such a dive, but there really isn't a reason. Leave her in peace. In 1980 the Cousteau divers made a very brief filming dive in their manned submersible. Some of the resulting footage was included in a film about the Great Lakes and the St. Lawrence River.

It is as songwriter Gordon Lightfoot so aptly put it in his ballad, "The Wreck of the EDMUND FITZ-GERALD."

"With a load of iron ore, 26,000 tons more.
Than the EDMUND FITZGERALD weighted empty,
That good ship and true was a bone to be chewed.
When the gales of November came early"

REFERENCES:

National Transportation Safety Board, Marine Accident
Report, S.S. EDMUND FITZGERALD Sinking in Lake
Superior, 10 November 1975., May 4, 1978.
United States Department of Transportation, Marine
Casualty Report, S.S. EDMUND FITZGERALD; Sinking
in Lake Superior on 10 November 1975 with Loss of
Life, U.S. Coast Guard Marine Board of Investigation
Report and Commandant's Action, 26 July 1977.

ADDITIONAL ACCIDENTS

1853   BALTIMORE, steamer, ashore near Whitefish Point, $2,000 in damages.

1857   LAMPLIGHTER, schooner, stranded at Whitefish Point.

1858   GENERAL TAYLOR, propeller, collided with brig CONCORD near Whitefish Point.

1864   IRON CITY, propeller, struck reef and sank in Waiska Bay, recovered.

       CLEVELAND, steamer, wrecked at Two Hearted River, total loss of $35,000.

1865   LADY FRANKLIN, propeller, sank in Waiska Bay with $13,000 in damages, recovered.

1866   JOHN A. DIX, stranded on a reef near Whitefish Point, recovered.

1868   WARRINGTON, steamer, disabled in a gale off Whitefish Point.

1869   E.R. BLAKE, schooner, ashore in a gale at Whitefish Point, recovered.

       NUCLEUS, bark, ore cargo, sunk off Whitefish Point.

1870   SOUTHWEST, schooner, ore cargo, ashore at Vermilion Point, recovered.

       LOTTIE WOLF, schooner, disabled in a gale near Whitefish Point.

F. SIEGEL, schooner, ashore at Vermilion Point, recovered.

1872 UNION, propeller, ashore at Whitefish Point, recovered.

CASCADE, schooner, ashore at Whitefish Point, recovered.

ST. PAUL, propeller, disabled in a gale off Whitefish Point.

FEARLESS, schooner, sprang a leak off Whitefish Point.

1873 MASSILION, bark, ore cargo, ashore at Whitefish Point, recovered.

1874 JARVIS LORD, steamer, disabled off Whitefish Point.

HARVEST HOME, schooner, with ore, stranded at Waiska Bay, recovered.

ROCKET, propeller, with ore, stranded at Waiska Bay, recovered.

1875 PACIFIC, propeller, ashore at Point Iroquois, recovered.

SUMATRA, schooner, ashore at Big Two Hearted River, recovered.

1876 CONSTITUTION, with coal, ashore at Whitefish Point, recovered.

NAHANT, propeller, ashore at Waiska Bay, recovered.

The propeller PACIFIC. She was briefly ashore at Point Iroquois.

1877 CHARLIE, schooner, lost near Grand Marais.

1878 TREMPE, barge with ore, ashore ten miles east of Grand Marais.

CITY OF FREMONT, propeller, struck a reef near Whitefish Point, recovered.

E.M. PECK, tug damaged in a gale at Whitefish Point.

ST. MARIES, steamer, ashore nine miles east of Grand Marais in a snow storm, recovered.

1880 W.B. CASTLE, tug, sprung a leak near Whitefish Point, recovered.

ANNIE M. PETERSON, schooner, ashore at Whitefish Point, recovered.

JOHN KELDERHOUSE, schooner, grounded at Waiska Bay, recovered.

1881 NEGAUNEE, schooner, disabled in a squall off Whitefish Point, recovered.

THOS. QUEYLE, schooner, disabled in a squall off Whitefish Point, recovered.

In 1878 the propeller CITY OF FREMONT struck a reef off Whitefish Point. As pictured, she is being repaired in a floating drydock, not necessarily as a result of the Whitefish Point incident.

Lake Superior Marine Museum

1882 GRACE, steamer, ashore at Whitefish Point with loss of two lives, recovered.

ONTARIO, propeller, lost 400 barrels of flour off Whitefish Point.

PEARL, scow, wrecked at Whitefish Point.

213

ARAXAS, steam barge, sank in Waiska Bay after developing a leak, recovered.

1883 J.R. WHITLING, propeller, with lumber, disabled at Whitefish Point, recovered.

WABASH, schooner, wrecked attempting to enter Grand Marais harbor during storm.

1884 MEARS, barge, stranded at Whitefish Point, recovered.

PACIFIC, propeller, stranded at Whitefish Point, recovered.

SPARTA, steamer, ashore at Point Iroquois, recovered.

NEGAUNEE, schooner, with ore, stranded in Waiska Bay, recovered.

WHITE STAR, schooner, with ore, stranded in Waiska Bay, recovered.

WINSLOW, tug, stranded in Waiska Bay, recovered.

JOHN MARTIN, schooner, ashore at Whitefish Point, recovered.

1885 SANDUSKY, schooner, with coal, ashore at Whitefish Point, recovered.

1887 ARGONAUT, steamer, aground near Crisp Point, recovered.

JAY GOULD, steamer, grounded at Whitefish Point as a result of smoke from a forest fire, recovered.

WALLUDA, steamer, grounded on Pancake Shoal, recovered.

CHARLEMAGNE TOWER JR., steam barge, grounded at Waiska Bay, recovered.

PENDILL, tug, ashore above Whitefish Point, recovered.

HANCOCK, tug ashore at Parisienne Island in storm, recovered.

1888 H.B. TUTTLE, steam barge and QUEEN CITY, schooner-barge, ashore at Crisp Point in fog, recovered.

D. BALLENTINE, steamer, aground in Waiska Bay, recovered.

1889 SPECULAR, steamer, aground in Waiska Bay, recovered.

1890 June 3 OLYMPIA, steamer, aground near Whitefish Point, recovered.

August 15 Yacht RAMONA sunk after collision with tug JOHN HICKLER, recovered.

1891, May 17 ADVANCE, steamer ashore at Whitefish Bay in a fog, recoverd.

June 11 GEORGE G. HADLEY, wooden steamer ashore at Whitefish Point, recovered.

September 25 MABEL WILSON, schooner, ashore at Crisp Point.

September 29 BETHA ENDRESS, tug, foundered off Whitefish Point in a gale with the loss of five men.

October 2 CHINA, passenger steamer, aground at Pancake Shoal, recovered.

1893 CLARA BELLE, steamer, lost upper works in a fire while moored in Grand Marais harbor.

CENTURION, steamer, stranded near Waiska Bay, recovered.

May 14 NIPIGON, steamer, DELAWARE, MELBOURNE, schooner-barges, ashore near Vermilion Point in a fog, recovered.

August 18 MARINA, steam barge, ashore at Whitefish Point, recovered.

September 30 MYSTIC, tug, burned to water's edge near Taquamenon Bay.

1895 RICHARD J. CARNEY, steamer, aground at Shelldrake, recovered.

HATTIE, schooner-barge, ashore at Grand Marais, recovered.

May 14 JOHN J. BARLUM, schooner-barge, ashore at Two Hearted River in storm, recovered.

June 14 WILLIAM H. GRATWICK, steel steamer, ashore at Point Iroquois, recovered.

September 4 CUMBERLAND, steamer, ashore at Whitefish Point, recovered.

October 8 ABERDEEM, schooner-barge, ashore at Point Iroquois in storm, recovered.

October 19 COL. ELLSWORTH, schooner-barge, ashore at Whitefish Point, recovered.

October 31 NELLIE TORRENT, schooner-barge and BROCKWAY, tug, ashore at Point Iroquois, recovered.

1896, July 27 SAVELAND, schooner-barge, ashore at Vermilion Point, recovered.

November 2 H.W. SIBLEY, steamer, ashore at Grand Marais in storm, recovered.

SAMSON, steamer, aground at Bay Mills, recovered.

1897, July 11 SIR WILLIAM FAIRBORN, steel steamer, GEORGE H. CORLISS, schooner-barge, ashore at Waiska Bay, recovered.

July 26 E.A. SHORES, wooden steamer, aground at Point Iroquois, recovered.

October 28 R.J. HACKETT, schooner-barge, aground in Waiska Bay, recovered.

1898, September 20 ORR, steel steamer and CARRINGTON, schooner, aground at Waiska Bay, recovered.

September MONITOR, lighter, sunk with the loss of five men off Point Iroquois.

September 30 WAVERLY, steamer, ashore at Whitefish Point, recovered.

1899, May 21 H.B. RUNNELS, steamer, ashore near Grand Marais, recovered.

May 25 A.D. THOMASON, whaleback steamer, stranded Waiska Bay, recovered.

June 3 GRIFFIN, steamer, rammed and sunk by steamer WAWATAM in a fog off Point Iroquois.

1900, November 18 PERRY and COMPANY, 100 ton barge, swamped in northwest gale three miles east of Grand Marais, five lives lost.

1901, June 29 AVON, 251 foot wooden steamer, badly damaged by a fire off Point Aux Pins.

October 8 JULIA LARSON, schooner, storm damaged one-half mile northeast of Grand Marais, assistance needed.

October 8 J.W. WESCOTT, 18 ton steam tug, sank in Grand Marais harbor.

November 8 KEWEENAW, 493 ton schooner, sank in Grand Marais harbor, recovered.

November 10 TEMPEST, steamer, stranded in Grand Marais harbor.

1902, July 28 SEA GULL, yacht, disabled off Grand Marais, recovered.

September 17 JOHN B. WELBOR, schooner, sank in Grand Marais harbor when pumps became disabled.

1903, June 25 MARION, gas launch, lost screw off Crisp Point, recovered.

Sailboat, sank in northwest gale one-half mile east of Grand Marais, one life lost.

1904, April 7 MONARCH, steamer, struck 12 miles above Whitefish Point in fog, recovered.

April 7 WISCONSIN, steamer, grounded in a fog near Vermilion Point, recovered.

June 30 TIONESTA, steamer, ashore at Whitefish Point in fog, recovered.

August 5 MARION, gas launch, disabled off Vermilion, assisted by Life-Savers.

August 16 CHARLES R. VAN HISE, steamer, stranded at Whitefish Point, recovered.

September 28 J. DUVALL, schooner, lost in south gale one-quarter mile north of Grand Marais.

1905, May 16 SYLVANIA, SIR HENRY BESSEMER, steel steamers, collide off Whitefish Point with $10,000 damages to SYLVANIA and $50,000 to the BESSEMER.

June 9 GEORGE B. LEONARD, steel steamer, aground at Point Iroquois, recovered.

September 3 GEORGE STEPHENSON, steel steamer, aground at Point Aux Pins, recovered.

November 20 PORTAGE, wooden steamer, ashore at Grand Marais, recovered.

1906, May 17 TROY, JAMES GAYLEY, steamers, collided in fog in Whitefish Bay, recovered.

September 14 TEMPEST, steamer, stranded on Tahquamenon Island Reef, recovered.

1907, April 25 WILLIAM A PAYNE, JOSEPH G. BUTLER, JR., steel steamers, collide in Whitefish Bay fog, recovered.

July 10 B.B. BUCKOUT, schooner-barge, ashore at Crisp Point, recovered.

July 10 J. RIDDLE, steamer, aground in Whitefish Bay, recovered.

July 13 SAXONA, CITY OF BANGOR, steel steamers, collide in Whitefish Bay fog, recovered.

1908, July 10 J. RIDDLE, steamer, stranded in White-fish Bay during fog, recovered.

December 6 STANTON, steamer, stranded during a snow storm off Point Iroquois, recovered.

1909, April 26 PHILLIP MINCH, E.Y. TOWNSEND, steel steamers, collided off Whitefish Point with minor damage.

May 29 GLORIANA, yacht, destroyed by fire in Grand Marais.

August 9 WILLIAM A. HAWGOOD, steel steamer, ashore at Vermilion Point in a fog, recovered.

October 19 ALEXANDER HOLLEY, whaleback barge, SUPERIOR CITY, steel steamer, collided in Whitefish Bay with minor damage.

November 16 PAISLEY, schooner-barge, lost deck cargo of lumber in gale off Crisp Point.

1910, April 21 LYCOMING, steamer, ashore at Grand Marais, recovered.

October 28 MANITOU, steamer, ashore at Grand Marais, recovered.

December 9 ETHEL J., steamer, sank at dock in Grand Marais harbor after cutting hull on ice, recovered.

1911, June 6 FRANK J. HECKLER, steel steamer, ashore two miles east of the Two Hearted River, recovered.

1913, April 22 CALDERA, A.E. STEWART, steel steamers collide in ice in Whitefish Bay, minor damage.

April 23 CAPTAIN THOMAS WILSON, steel steamer, broke three propeller bladed in Whitefish Bay ice, disabled, recovered.

May 13 SIERRA, steamer, breaks propeller blade in Whitefish Bay ice, disabled, recovered.

June 20 CHOCTAW, steamer, strands in Waiska Bay, recovered.

October 6 MONARCH, 42 foot gas launch, destroyed by fire in Grand Marais harbor.

1915, September 6 CLARENCE A. BLACK, JOHN DUNN JR., steamers, collide in fog in Whitefish Bay, recovered.

1916, April 28 WILLIAM NOTTINGHAM, WILLIAM A. ROGERS, steel steamers, collide in Whitefish Bay, recovered.

May 8 DELOS W. COOKE, steamer, broke three propeller blades in Whitefish Bay ice, disabled, recovered.

July 27 WILLIAM NOTTINGHAM, W. GRANT, steel steamers, collided northwest of Whitefish Point, recovered.

1917, May 3 N.F. LEOPOLD, steamer, struck an unknown object in Whitefish Bay ice field, recovered.

May 7 DANIEL J. MORRELL, steel steamer, collided with steel steamer VULCAN in Whitefish Bay ice field, recovered.

May 10 JOHN OWEN, steamer, aground at Corbeil Point, recovered.

May 16 HARRY COULBY, steel steamer, damaged in Whitefish Bay ice field.

May 21 G.A. TOMILSON, steel steamer, damaged in Whitefish Bay ice field, recovered.

1918, April 28 ARGUS, steel steamer, damaged in ice off Crisp Point.

May 3 E.L. PIERCE, steamer damaged in ice field off Whitefish Point.

May 6 GRANVILLE A. RICHARDSON, steel steamer, damaged in Whitefish Point ice field.

May 6 J.J. SULLIVAN, steel steamer, damaged in ice field off Whitefish Point.

May 7 A.A. AUGUSTUS, steel steamer, damaged hull in ice field off Crisp Point.

May 19 D.M. PHILBIN, BELGIUM, steamers collided northwest of Whitefish Point, recovered.

1919, October 30 CHARLES H. BRADLEY, wooden steamer, while upbound in Whitefish Bay, struck an unseen object, damaged propeller, recovered.

1920, April 30 LACROSSE, steel steamer, ashore at Parisienne Island, recovered.

June 12 B. LYMAN, F.R. HAZARD, steamers, collided 15 miles northwest of Whitefish Point, recovered.

November 12 FRANCIS L. ROBBINS, steamer, 25 miles north of Whitefish Point a heavy sea boarded the steamer and swept away her pilothouse.

1921, November 11 P.J. RALPH, 211 foot steamer, grounded west of Grand Marais in a storm.

1922, November 23 E.J. EARLING, steamer, suffered severe damage in heavy weather west of Whitefish Point.

1923, May 6 J. LEONARD REPOGLE, EDWIN E. SLICK, steel steamers, collided in Whitefish Bay ice field, recovered.

May 11 ARTHUR E. NEWBOLD, LUPUS, steamers, collided in Whitefish Bay ice field, recovered.

May 12 R.L. AGASSIZ, steel steamer, grounded near Point Iroquois while moving in ice field.

July 12 THOMAS WALTERS, steel steamer, broke propeller near Whitefish Point.

July 23 HORACE S. WILKINSON, WILLIAM B. SCHILLER, steel steamers, collided in fog near Point Iroquois, both heavily damaged.

October 11 JOHN MCCARTNEY KENNEDY, HENRY STEINBRENNER, steel steamers, collided in Whitefish Bay fog, recovered.

October 13 DENMARK, steel steamer, broke propeller when it struck an unknown object near Whitefish Point.

1924, July 24 AMASA, MERTON E. FARR, steel steamers, collided in a fog near Parisienne Island, recovered.

1925 September 19 A.E.R. SCHNEIDER, steel steamer, damaged after striking an unknown object near Whitefish Point.

October 19 MONROE C. SMITH, steel steamer, damaged after striking an unknown object in Whitefish Bay.

1927 December 2 DANIEL J. MORRELL, S.H. ROBBINS, steel steamer, collided near Point Iroquois, recovered.

1928, May 3 CHARLES S. HEBARD, LAVALDOC, steel steamers, collided in Whitefish Bay ice field, minor damages.

June 27 A.H. STUART, 104 foot steamer, grounded west of Grand Marais, recovered.

July 24 KIOWA, steel steamer, grounded on west end of Parisienne Island in a fog, recovered with heavy damages.

August 3 FRED G. HARTWELL, JAMES E. FERRIS, steel steamers, collided east of Whitefish Point in fog, minor damages.

August 23 G.J. GRAMMER, WESTMOUNT, steel steamers, collided in a fog west of Whitefish Point, recovered.

1929, December 2 ALICE L., gas fish vessel, lost west of Grand Marais in northwest gale, one life lost.

1930, April 28 WEYBURN, FRONTENAC, steel steamers, collided in Whitefish Bay with minor damages.

May 2 MUNISING, steel steamer, grounded in a storm on Parisienne Island, recovered.

1933, April 10 Coast Guard Vessel, small boat, sunk in Whitefish Bay after being crushed by ice while on search mission for missing fisherman, crew rescued by Whitefish Point Lightkeeper.

1943, June 2   HARRY W. HOSFORD, W.W. HOLLOWAY, steel steamers, collided in Whitefish Bay, recovered.

1961, May 6   CRYSTALL JEWELL, 461 foot British freighter, aground on a reef off Gros Cap, recovered.

1964, September 26   MARKAY, 30 foot cabin cruiser, lost during squall five miles east of Whitefish Point.

1980, October 8   SALLIE, 42 foot gill netter, stranded on Whitefish Point, recovered.

Unknown   ORA ENDRESS, a launch that capsized in Whitefish Bay, Whitefish Point Lightkeeper rescued all 11 men aboard.

THE LIFE-SAVERS

Introduction

The history of the United States Life-Saving Service is long and reasonably complicated. The following history should not be considered complete, rather it is a sketch of the events that had major impact and a look at the "shipwreck coast" stations.

The story of the Life-Savers really began on the east coast of the United States, where a spectacular increase in wrecks and lives lost was causing great public concern. Government involvement in life-saving started in 1837 when an Act of Congress directed the old Revenue Cutter Service to make "seasonal cruises along the coast for the relief of distressed mariners." There was no provision for assistance from shore based stations.

As the terrible toll of shipwrecks increased, different solutions to the life-saving problem were tried, to include providing lighthouses with lifeboats and building and equipping life-saving stations, but manning them only with volunteers. In 1854, lifeboats were purchased for 46 volunteer stations, on Lakes Erie, Ontario and Michigan, but the complete lack of organization resulted in disuse, abuse and neglect.

Life-saving is difficult and dangerous work requiring the utmost in training and teamwork. Under the best of conditions, volunteer crews could not approach the degree of expertise required. These problems were brought harshly to the public attention during the winter of 1870-1871 when 214 people drowned in a shipwreck on the Great Lakes, many, it was claimed, as a direct result of poor equipment and untrained crews.

In response to the public outcry, Congress in April of 1871 authorized $200,000 for the purpose of erecting new stations, repairing equipment and paying crews. To administer the funds, the Secretary of the

Treasury established the Revenue Marine Bureau. Under it was the old Revenue Cutter Service and the brand new United States Life-Saving Service. Sumner I. Kimball was appointed head of the Bureau.

Sumner set to his task with a will. He reorganized the entire Bureau. Inefficient officers were removed, stations repaired, new equipment purchased, regulations issued that established the responsibility of crews and discipline was enforced. Strict qualifications for admission to the Service were established. A system of inspecting Stations for efficiency was developed. A special commission interviewed ship owners, insurance underwriters, vessel masters and wreckers to select sites for new stations.

A need was recognized for three distinct classes of stations;

A first class station contained all the equipment required to render aid to vessels in distress at isolated locations. Full-time crews would man the stations. Each station cost $5,302.

Second class stations as planned would be primary lifeboat stations only, with volunteer crews. These stations would be situated in populated areas where volunteers would be readily available, as well as assistance from local tugs and salvage operations. Each station cost $4,790.

The third class station, a house of refuge, was to be used only in Florida.

In 1874 Congress authorized 14 first class and 16 second class stations for the Great Lakes. Four of the first class stations were for Lake Superior. The actual locations were selected by Captain J.H. Merryman of the Revenue Marine in September 1874. Built in 1875, the stations at Vermilion Point, Crisp Point, Two Hearted River and Muskalonge Lake, (Deer Park) were operational in 1876.

Originally the Great Lakes was organized into three Life-Saving Districts: The Ninth, consisting of the coasts of Lakes Ontario and Erie; the Tenth, Lakes Huron and Superior and the Eleventh, Lake Michigan.

Later the Districts would be reorganized numerous times. Interestingly the District tradition is still kept up today since the Coast Guard on the Great Lakes is the Ninth Coast Guard District.

Kimball did his job so well that in 1878 the Life-Saving Service was made a separate organization under the Department of the Treasury. President Rutherford B. Hayes appointed Kimball as the General Superintendent, a position he held until 1915, a period of 37 years!

During this period the Life-Saving Service continued to grow. By 1893 there were 47 stations on the Great Lakes. In 1900 there were 60. While Kimball did much to reorganize the Service, it wasn't until 1896 that it was brought under the auspices of the new Civil Service system and any hint of political manipulation removed.

It was under the leadership of Kimball that the fledgling Life-Saving Service emerged as the stuff of legends. The popular press called its members "storm warriors" and "heroes of the surf." Newspapers and journals frequently carried stories of their courage, daring and heroism. By and large, these tales were true. It's been said that men are only as great as the challenge before them. If so, the early Life-Savers had plenty of opportunity to demonstrate their special skills. As the shipwreck section of this book illustrates, the carnage along the "shipwreck coast" was immense.

The Life-Savers remained in existence until 1915 when, under the threat of American involvement in a European war, it was combined with the Revenue Cutter Service into the present United States Coast Guard. Thus ended a glorious chapter in American maritime history. Although the traditions of the old Life-Saving Service continued for a short period in the fledging Coast Guard, the eventual retirement of the original Life-Savers, increased mechanization and a larger burden of official red tape slowly ended the legendary traditions of the "storm warriors."

Original Sites

Merryman's selection of the general location for the original four Lake Superior stations was doubtlessly influenced by the area's reputation as the "shipwreck coast."

In November of 1872, the losses of the schooners JUPITER, SATURN, CHARLES C. GRISWOLD and W.O. BROWN, all on the shipwreck coast, accounted for the death of all 29 crewmen and a property loss of $76,000. It was thought in marine quarters that if professional life-savers were present, lives could have been saved. This quadruple disaster also helped stimulate Congress into action.

One characteristic Merryman's sites had in common was isolation. The stations would be built on the edge of what was and still largely is primeval forest. There were no settlements, towns, or villages closer than Newberry, 35 miles distant from the Deer Park Station, the least isolated of the stations. This meant there were no schools, churches, doctors or stores. The stations were literally outposts of civilization on the edge of the vast wilderness. If the loneliness was bad during the navigation season when the crews were at the stations, it was devastating during the winter when only the keepers were required to remain. Sometimes their wives stayed with them and sometimes not.

The Men

Special care was given to the selection of the men who would man the stations. Although the rules for selection did occasionally change, they were always very stringent. The following general rules are typical of the care taken, but are by no means complete.

No man was accepted as a Surfman except upon examination and certification by the U.S. Civil Service Commission (effective 1896).

At least three years' experience was required, either as a surfman, sailor or boatman. Surfman meant experience in handling boats as a surf fisherman or wrecker. Each applicant had to provide two vouchers certifying that experience.

Ready with a heaving line, an old time Life-Saver poses for the camera.

Marquette Maritime Museum

He also had to have a certificate of his physical condition provided through an examination by a doctor of the U.S. Marine Hospital Service. If such a doctor was not available, an examination by a local doctor could be substituted if the doctor could be vouched for by the local station Keeper.

Applicants must be U.S. citizens, between the ages of 18 and 45, not less than 5 foot 6 inches in height; not less than 135 nor more than 205 pounds; must live in the district of their employment and not more than five miles inland from the shores of the Great Lakes, ocean or river; must be able to read and write English, and be a good swimmer.

The term of enlistment on the Great Lakes ran from the opening of navigation (April 15) until the close (December 15). The pay in 1906 was $65 a month for a Surfman and $75 a month for a Keeper. Keepers were usually paid for a full year and required to live at the stations. Surfmen had to fend for themselves during the off months. Many worked as lumberjacks in the nearby forests. In the spring all had to again apply for employment and take another physical. Any physical defect could rule them out, regardless of past employment. It was not unusual for men with 18 years of service not to be accepted. There was no retirement pension for service or injury. If he died in the line of duty, his family received no compensation.

The most important man was the Keeper, often referred to as the Captain. He had absolute authority over the crew and in the remote stations also served as the ex-officio customs inspector. He had responsibility for all shipwrecked property until recovered by the owner. Since he also lived at the station year around, he was responsible for its care and maintenance, as well as that of all the life-saving gear. When a boat was used in the rescue he manned the steering oar. The job called for remarkable leadership ability and there were those who became legends. As long as the Life-Saving Service will be remembered, Captains like Henry J. Cleary (Deer Park and Marquette), Benjamin Truedell (Grand Marais), Albert Ocha (Two Hearted River and Portage) and John Anderson (Two Hearted River) will live forever. These men cut their teeth on Superior's worst storms. They and their crews were certainly among the finest small boat handlers the world has ever seen.

The Lake Superior stations usually had nine man crews, the Keeper plus eight Surfmen. It was exactly enough to man the largest boat at the station and no more. The Life-Saving Service had no room for frills.

The Surfmen were ranked by order of skill and experience, the Number One Surfman being the most competent and Number Eight the least. Every man had his number stitched to his left sleeve. For every drill in the manual, each man had a specific job to do and it was strictly by "the numbers."

There was upward mobility within the crews. As a man left, he was often replaced by the man below, until eventually the Number Eight was always the newest man. Often, when the Keeper left, his place was taken by the Number One. If the Keeper was absent for any reason, it was the Number One who assumed command.

It wasn't until 1889 that uniforms were required. Until then the men usually used a local variant. Even when the Service required uniforms, the men still had to pay for them. A Surfman's uniform cost $15, a Keeper's $20.

Daily Operations, General

While the popular press may have given the impression that the Life-Saver's daily life was filled with dangerous and thrilling rescues, such was not the case. Every day, except Sunday, would be spent maintaining gear or drilling. Two drills were particularly popular with spectators.

The Beach Apparatus

The first of the popular drills was the beach apparatus drill. The Life-Saving Service considered it so important that regulations required it to be practiced twice a week, on Monday and Thursday. The drill was to be completed in not more than five minutes, but many crews were able to achieve a time of two minutes. The rivalry and competition between different crews was fierce, but what developed was a very high degree of professionalism and teamwork. In the midst of a hell blown Superior gale, when every minute counted and a mistake could spell death for the Life-Savers and shipwrecked alike, the men would do their jobs.

The beach apparatus was the primary means of rescue for vessels within 600 yards of the shore, the maximum range of the Lyle gun. The apparatus consisted of a small bronze cannon (weight 185 pounds) known as a Lyle gun, named for the Army Ordnance officer who developed it; a shot line and faking box (80 pounds); three 17-pound line shot; one set of two and one-half inch hauling lines or whip with block (300 pounds); a four and one-half inch hawser (600 pounds) and a crotch and sand anchor (125 pounds). As time passed, there were some variations to this list. Together the equipment normally weighed in excess of 1,340 pounds. All of it was carried on a small wagon known as a "beach cart." Usually it was pulled by the men, although on some occasions it was hauled by a horse team.

As this illustration from the Life-Saving Service instruction book shows, the beach drill was performed "by the numbers."

Author's Collection

The entire drill was done "by the book," with each step and who was responsible for it being carefully spelled out. At each command from the Keeper, the specific Surfman knew exactly what his job was. Quoting from the manual for example, on the first command, "Open boat room doors, Man the beach cart," No. 5 and 6 open and secure the boat room doors. If necessary to run the boat out, No. 1 and 2 ship the pole of the boat wagon, No. 1 holding the pole, No. 2 inserting the bolt. The crew run out the boat, No. 1 and No. 2 guiding the pole." There was no doubt in any man's mind as to what his job was.

Each station had a special exercise area established for the drill. The most important feature was the drill pole, a tall pole with a set of wooden cross arms on top simulating a vessel's mast and yards.

Briefly speaking, when the crew reached the wreck site, the various lines were carefully laid out and Lyle gun setup. After selecting a proper charge and aiming the gun, a light messenger line would be fired out to the wreck (or drill pole). Aboard the vessel the shipwrecked sailors would use the light line to haul out a heavier whip line about one-half inch thick. This line had a pulley through which the line passes back to the beach. Also with the doubled line is a small piece of wood with printed instructions.

The pulley is made fast to some substantial part of the wreck, usually a mast. Through the pulley the Life-Savers ashore haul a heavier two and one-half inch hawser. The heavier line is also secured to the wreck, as well as to shore. When possible, it was tied off to a tree or rock, but along Superior's sandy coast, a sand anchor was normally used. Near the water's edge a wooden frame or cross was raised under the line to lift it clear of the waves. Using a travelling line, a breeches buoy consisting of a cork life ring with a set of short canvas breeches (thus the name) sewed into it would be hauled out to the wreck. One by one, dangling high above the waves, the Life-Savers would bring the shipwreck survivors ashore.

In some instances a life-car, an enclosed metal capsule about eight feet long and four feet wide, could be used in place of the breeches buoy. Up to four people could ride the car at once, but it was only rarely, if ever used along the Lake Superior coast. This writer has been unable to find a single instance of its' use.

Boat Drill

The other drill that was popular with spectators was normally practiced on Tuesdays. It consisted of beach launching the surfboat through the breakers and working in the surf for at least 30 miles. Then the boat would be capsized with the crew quickly righting it and continue rowing. The purpose of the drill was to completely condition the crew to react properly when the boat went over during an actual rescue. The crews became so proficient that the boat would roll and right itself in nearly the same motion.

The drill was so popular with the public that crews often performed it at community celebrations and events. While the Surfmen always got wet, a good nimble footed Keeper was often able to scamper over the overturned hull without even getting his feet wet!

Special emphasis was placed on running the boat through the surf and safely landing on the beach. The Keepers regularly practiced with a drogue. Trailing the sea-anchor type device off the stern would keep the stern down and help prevent the surfboat from accidentally capsizing.

There were two boats primarily used by the Life-Savers. The first was a light, 700-1,000 pound self-bailing, self-righting surfboat. On Lake Superior prior to 1915, this was the 25 foot Beebe-McLellan surfboat. This was the boat that was nearly always used when a launch through the surf was necessary. The second boat was the big 30-36 foot, two to four ton, self-righting, self-bailing lifeboat. It was generally used when a launching could be made from the station where it was kept on permanent launch-way. Initially, the big lifeboat was rowed, but as a result of a successful 1899 experiment between the Marquette Life-Saving Station and the Lake Shore Engine Company, the decision was made to motorize the fleet. By 1908, virtually all lifeboats were motorized.

This photograph of the Marquette Life-Saving crew (circa 1893) graphically shows the difference between a lifeboat (at left) and a surfboat (at right).

Marquette County Historical Society

It should be realized that both the beach apparatus and surfboat drills were not practiced just on warm summer days. Rather they were performed in the best and worst of weather. Shipwrecks typically happened when the storms roared full on the lake and that was also the time the Life-Savers honed their critical skills.

Under a cloud of cold spray, a Coast Guard motor lifeboat speeds through the surf!

Other Drills and Duties

The remainder of the Life-Saver's week was spent on a variety of drills. Signal drill consisted of each Surfman becoming proficient in the various "wig wag" flag signals. The men became so skilled that many were transferred to the Army Signal Corps during the Spanish American War.

Additional time was spent practicing the "restoration of the apparently drowned," an early method of resuscitation. The Surfman were also trained in the use of the station medicine kit as well as first aid.

The crews spent Saturday in general maintenance of all the equipment as well as the building and grounds. There was always work to be done, some piece of equipment to be checked. The men knew that their lives often depended on how well that equipment was maintained.

There were also continuous duties to be performed. Each station had a lookout tower in which a day watch was constantly kept. No seats were allowed in the tower, which meant the lookout had to remain alert. He couldn't fall asleep sitting down. In addition every half hour the lookout rang a bell to let the Captain know that all was well and he was still awake. A careful log was kept of all vessels passing the station and the condition of wind and sea.

The Surfmen lived at the station and were on call 24 hours a day. Married men could eat at home, but were required to sleep at the station to be ready for any call. Minutes lost while a surfman returned from his wife's warm bed could spell the difference between life and death.

Beach Patrol

In addition to the day watch, night beach patrols were also made. The patrols were divided into four basic watches, sunset to 8 p.m., 8 p.m. to 12 p.m., 12 p.m. to 4 a.m. and 4 a.m. to sunrise. For example, the patrolmen at Vermilion, leaving at sunset, would walk the short patrol, two miles to the east and west, one man in each direction. When they returned at 8 p.m., the next two men walked the long patrol, four miles each day.

The patrols were long, lonely affairs. Often in the spring and fall, the beaches were "clad with ice." At other times, "pathless deserts in the night." Regardless of the weather, the patrols were always made. A full norther' could be savaging the lake, but still the lone Life-Saver walked his patrol.

If the stations were too far apart for the two patrols to meet, the patrolman carried a time clock. When he reached the end of his patrol, he would find a key on the limit post. Turning the key in the clock would mark the exact time he reached his limit. He would then make the return patrol to the station.

Later, small shelter huts with telephones were built behind the dunes. Instead of using a time clock, the beach patrol would call in. Eventually all of the stations were linked together by the thin wires.

If the Surfman had a short patrol, two miles in each direction, he only had a pleasant four mile hike. If he had a long patrol, four miles each way, then his night's walk was eight miles. Often every step was in sand. The trail he followed was varied. In some places it ran right on the beach. In others it wandered along the top of the sand banks. When the weather was clear, visibility from the top of the dunes was excellent.

If he spotted a vessel in distress or heading for shore, he would burn a Coston signal. A Coston was a special brilliant red flare that could be seen for ten miles.

A Life-Saver on beach patrol (circa 1900).

Marquette Maritime Museum

The lonely beach patrolman was the cause of many a dramatic rescue. It was he who first saw the wreck on the bar, or discovered a half-dead sailor washed ashore. Running back to the station, his breathless report would set the wheels of rescue into action.

Regardless of how long or difficult his patrol, or how tired he was, the patrolman was required to participate in the rescue effort. Every man was needed. There was no one to take his place.

One of the depressing aspects of the Life-Savers job was recovering the bodies of shipwreck sailors. Some, called "floaters," were picked up offshore. This was comparatively rare. Usually they washed up on the shore and were discovered by the beach patrol.

The usual procedure, especially in the early days, was for the Keeper to make careful note of the physical description of the body, assuming there was no identification on it and then bury it in a marked grave high on the banks. The information would be wired to headquarters, as well as to the vessel owner if there was an identified wreck. If the body was claimed, it was shipped back. If not, it stayed right where it was.

One of the old Two Hearted River crew remembered that half way between Deer Park and Two Hearted River, there was a small forested ridge running into the open beach. Located on the ridge was a simple wooden cross marking the final resting place of a sailor known only as "sailor Jack." What wreck he came from was never known, but when the beach patrols passed, they always paid their respects.

For bodies that came ashore during warm weather, burial was certainly the best answer. But sometimes there were variations. In November, 1919, the big steamer JOHN OWEN sank with all 22 hands somewhere between the Keweenaw and Whitefish Point. The following March the Crisp Point Coast Guard discovered the body of the assistant engineer encased in a cake of ice. The station kept the body in its own "wrap around cooler" and notified the OWEN's owners. But as the days passed and no word was received and the find began to defrost, it was finally buried at the station.

Other Work

The Life-Savers were not called out just for the major rescues. They also rendered a variety of assistance to mariners.

Most common was helping to run towing hawsers for vessels aground and delivering telegrams requesting tugs. They also piloted vessels over local sand bars, especially at Deer Park. When the surf was too high for a vessel's yawl to land, the Life-Savers would come out to deliver or land passengers. If it concerned the lake, in one way or another, the station crews were involved.

The Life-Savers on the shipwreck coast sometimes had strange pets. Shown here is a pet timber wolf that was reportedly very playful unless it was feeding time.

Marquette Maritime Museum

Stations

The stations themselves could best be described as "functional." As typified the Service they were not fancy. Most stations originally were two story frame buildings. The bottom floor had a boat/apparatus room, mess room, store room and Keeper's room. The second floor had a crew room and a cot room for sheltering shipwrecked sailors. The lookout tower was either free standing or incorporated as part of the roof. Later, the stations were modified to include separate Keeper's quarters, and boat houses, cabins for the families of married Surfmen (at least for the Number One Surfman) and a separate mess house. Unmarried men still stayed in a bunk room.

Towns became very proud of "their" crews. The men were local people with families and homes. The Keepers were well respected for their special knowledge and skills. Often consulted on public issues, their opinion held much weight. In every facet, the stations were an integral part of the community.

CRISP POINT STATION

This Life-Saving Station, originally known as Station Number 10, was placed in operation in 1876. It took its name from the first Keeper, an iron-willed boatman named Christopher Crisp. Early records often refer to it as "Crisp's" Point, in reference to the old Keeper.

A visitor in 1892 described the location as "... a wilder looking place than the last (Vermilion). Tall, somber fir and pine trees in gloomy ranks reared their plumed heads beside the silent lake for miles away. The station house and the two or three cabins standing in the clearing beside it had a lonesome look on the edge of the endless forest."

Other than the station, "a long log house nearby answered the purpose of a boatroom and kitchen, the lower underground portion stowing the boats, for which are ways running to the water's edge. A cabin was

The Crisp Point Station (circa 1953). Note the large ice banks.

National Archives and Records Service

It is quite possible that the Crisp Point Station was initially built too close to the water. After roaring Superior storms threatened to wash it away, it was moved further inland. One old Surfman recollected it had been moved three times, the last time placing it even with the lighthouse. Based on today's observations, erosion has been severe. The Crisp Point Light itself is now nearly in water!

Today there is no apparent evidence of the old Life-Saving Station. Nature has reclaimed the site.

DEER PARK STATION

The Deer Park Station also known as Muskalonge

243

Lake Station, was originally officially designated as Station Number 12. It was placed in operation in 1876.

The Deer Park Station before being dismantled. Note the lookout tower above the right chimney.

Marquette Maritime Museum

In 1882 the Station had a log boathouse with a launchway running directly into the lake. A second log building served as a combination mess room and kitchen. An old Surfman at the Station remembered that the mess room was an especially drafty building, but he always thought it was purposely built that way to encourage quick eating. If it was uncomfortable enough, too much time would not be wasted over merely eating.

The original Keeper, an old sailor named Quinton Morgan, was a particularly rough hewn character. During the winter, he would stay at the Station alone, his only companions being a dog, cat and cow. Reportedly, when the crew returned in the spring, the cow often walked the night patrols with the Surfmen.

Deer Park Station (circa 1886). Note the launchway for the surfboat.

Captain Morgan kept a team of sled dogs for use during the winters. He made good use of the dogs during the summer also. He had trained them to roam the beaches during foggy nights, their loud baying serving as an unusual, but reportedly effective, fog horn.

Morgan often had trouble with his crews. His men were drawn from local lumberjacks and were especially rough cut. The Keeper insisted on strict discipline. To enforce his commands, Morgan carried a revolver with him at all times. For good measure, when he rode the surfboat, not only was the gun in his pocket, but a hatchet on the seat beside him. As the story goes, he was ready to use both.

GRAND MARAIS STATION

The Grand Marais Station was among the newest of the Lake Superior Life-Saving Stations, being established in 1900. By 1935, the Station had answered 700 cases of assistance, the vast majority minor affairs.

The Grand Marais Life-Saving Station (circa 1905). Each man wore his "number" on his left sleeve. Keeper Truedell is at the left. In this station the lookout tower was incorporated into the main building. The signal bell is plainly visible between the upper tower windows.

Michigan State Archives

The Station successfully made the transition from Life-Saving Station to Coast Guard Station and was an active facility until only very recently. Presently it is operated by the Coast Guard Auxilary, although part of the facility has been turned over to the Pictured Rocks National Lakeshore.

The original building was torn down in the 1930s. The present structure was constructed across the street from the old Station.

Grand Marais Coast Guard Station (circa 1945). The lake is choked with ice. The harbor entrance is in the foreground.

National Archives and Records Service

The Station's most influential Keeper was Benjamin Truedell. This legendary Keeper placed the Station in commission in 1900 and lead the crews until 1923.

The Grand Marais crew performing the surfboat drill. Stacks of cut lumber are visible in the background.

Lake Superior Marine Museum

One of the unique aspects of the Grand Marais Station was that the crew named their motor lifeboat. Time and time again, the Grand Marais crew sped to the rescue in the AUDACITY. Given the station's record of dangerous rescues, it certainly was a fitting name.

TWO HEARTED RIVER STATION

The Two Hearted River Station, originally known as Station Number 11, was placed in operation in 1876. Until its closing, Coast Guard records indicate 960 persons were assisted by the Station.

In 1882 the Station crew was composed almost entirely of Frenchmen, under the command of Keeper Moses Chartier. Reportedly, in deference to the one or two Americans in the crew, Chartier insisted that English be used whenever the crew was together.

The old Two Hearted River Life-Saving Station is long gone, except for a State of Michigan historical marker.

The Station was located on the west side of the Two Hearted River. The river curved such that it flowed directly behind the Station, thus it was common to moor the surfboat at a dock built out from the river bank.

The Station, like all of the old Lake Superior Life-Saving Stations, had a cemetery. Located on a hill southeast of the Station, it was the final resting place not just for shipwrecked sailors, but also for Surfmen and their families. Disease took a terrible toll at the isolated facilites. Far from any medical care, there was little that could be done for the sick. Buried in this small lonely plot are the remains of Mrs. Albert Ocha, the wife of Keeper Albert Ocha, and several of their children. Ocha was one of the legendary Keepers of the era.

On the lonely beach in front of the Two Hearted Station remnants of shipwreck can still be found, as this piece of machinery testifies.

Author's Collection

Another of the great Two Hearted River Keepers was John A. Anderson. For many years the Marquette's Station's Number One Surfman, he learned his trade under the expert tutelage of the illustrious Henry J. Cleary. From October 1912 until November 1915, he was the Keeper of the lonely Station. To battle the isolation, especially during the winters, Anderson built small dorys for sale to other Life-Savers and local fishermen. The extra money was a welcome supplement to his meager salary.

Today the only evidence of the old Station is the foundation of the buildings and some pilings on the river banks. Unlike the other original Stations, there is also a State of Michigan plaque commemorating the old Life-Savers.

The Two Hearted River Coast Guard crew rowing in their surfboat. Note the six man rowing crew, reduced from the original eight of the Life-Saving Service days The station house is visible on shore.

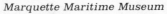

Marquette Maritime Museum

Life at a Life-Saving Station wasn't all work. Keeper John Anderson of the Two Hearted River Station proudly displays the results of a fishing trip.

Anderson Collection
Marquette Maritime
Museum

251

VERMILION POINT STATION

Considered the most isolated Station on Lake Superior, the Vermilion Point Station was placed in operation in 1876. Originally known as Station Number 9, it was the first Station reached after rounding Whitefish Point heading west.

The Vermilion Point Life-Saving Station (circa 1906). The exercise pole is visible in the foreground.

During the 1930s, the Station was home for six Coast Guardsmen and their families. The isolation was still severe. During the winters, the mail, as well as any passengers and supplies, were delivered to the Station via dog sled. It was a difficult ten-mile trip from Whitefish Point, taking on the average eight hours to complete.

Up until June 30, 1935, the Station responded to 1,003 calls for assistance, involving the lives of 900 persons. As in the case of the Grand Marais Station, the vast majority of the calls were of an extremely minor nature. Regretfully, more complete data are not available.

Today many of the buildings of the original Station are in ruins, the victims of time and vandalism. One building still standing is a two-story frame structure, 20 feet by 40 feet, probably dating from the original Station.

Looking west at the old Vermilion Point Life-Saving Station. The cedar shake buildings to the right and left are part of newer Coast Guard construction.

Author's Collection

The old Vermilion Point Life-Saving Station. This building is likely the original 1876 structure.

253   *Author's Collection*

WHITEFISH POINT STATION

The Whitefish Point Station was established in 1923. Unlike the original four stations and Grand Marais, it was never a United States Life-Saving Service facility, but rather, had always been a Coast Guard one. In 1915 the Life-Saving Service was combined with the Revenue Marine to form the Coast Guard. The Station was closed in 1970 when Whitefish Point Light was automated.

As of June 30, 1935, the Station had responded to 240 calls for assistance, and rendered aid to 77 persons. Since these numbers stand in sharp contrast to the Vermilion and Two Hearted River figures, one set or the other are perhaps suspect.

The Whitefish Point Coast Guard Station lookout tower. Long abandoned, it stands as a lonely sentinel of a by-gone age.

Author's Collection

The Station was located on the same grounds with the Whitefish Point Light. The lookout tower was and still is, on the east side of the Point. The Coast Guard Life-Saving crew was consolidated with the Lighthouse crew in 1947.

The Whitefish Point Coast Guard Station (circa 1930). The station building is at the left, lookout tower in the center and the light tower at the right.

Marquette Maritime Museum

REFERENCES:

Bennett, Robert F. *SURFBOATS, ROCKETS AND CARRONADES.* (Washington D.C.: U.S. Government Printing Office).

Bibb, A.B. "The Life-Savers on the Great Lakes". *FRANK LESLIE's POPULAR MONTHLY*, April 1882.

Bogue, Margaret Beattle, and Palmer, Virginia A. *AROUND THE SHORES OF LAKE SUPERIOR: A GUIDE TO HISTORIC SITES.* University of Wisconsin Sea Grant College Program, 1979.

Giambara, Paul. *SURFMEN AND LIFESAVERS.* (Centerville Mass.: Scrimshaw Press, 1969).

Law, Rev. W.H. *HEROES OF THE GREAT LAKES.* (Detroit: 1906).

Law, Rev. William Hainstock. *THE LIFE-SAVERS OF*

THE GREAT LAKES; INCIDENTS AND EXPERIENCES AMONG THE LIFE-SAVERS IN LAKE HURON AND LAKE SUPERIOR. (Detroit: Winn and Hammond, 1902).

Nalty, Bernard C., Noble, Dennis L., Strobridge, Truman R., ed. *Wrecks, RESCUES AND INVESTIGATIONS. (Wilmington, Delaware: Scholarly Resources Inc., 1978).*

Noble, Dennis L. and O'Brien, T. Michael. *SENTINELS OF THE ROCKS. (Marquette, Michigan: Northern Michigan University Press, 1979).*

O'Brien, T. Michael. *GUARDIANS OF THE EIGHT SEA, A HISTORY OF THE COAST GUARD ON THE GREAT LAKES. 1976.*

ONE HUNDRED AND FORTY-FIFTH ANNIVERSARY CELEBRATION, ELEVENTH DISTRICT, U.S. COAST GUARD, 1935.

Splake, T. Kilgore. *SUPERIOR LAND LIGHTS. (Battle Creek, Michigan: Angst Productions, 1984).*

Wolff, Dr. Julius F. Jr. *"A Lake Superior Life-Saver Reminisces". INLAND SEAS, Summer, 1968.*

THE LIGHTHOUSES

General

The lights at Whitefish Point, Crisp Point, Point Iroquois and Isle Parisienne were, and still are, an integral part of the story of the area's maritime history. To gain a full understanding of the history, the reader must have some comprehension of the history of these specific lights, as well as an overall view of the lighthouses on the Great Lakes.

The government's involvement in safe navigation began early in America's history. The first lighthouse was established in 1716 at Little Brewster Island at the entrance to Boston Harbor. By 1789, there were a dozen active lights.

The first light apparently came to the Great Lakes in 1813 when a beacon was established at Fort Niagara on Lake Ontario, although that is doubted in some historical circles. The Presque Isle light on Lake Erie may have preceded it.

As commerce grew on the lakes, so did the number of lighthouses. By 1865 there were seven on Lake Ontario, 12 on Lake Huron, 26 on Lake Michigan and 15 on Lake Superior. Each light increased shipping safely by warning mariners of dangerous shores and clear of reefs and shoals.

Organization.

The remarkable growth was under the auspices of the Lighthouse Board. Organized in 1852 under the Secretary of the Treasury, its members were Presidential appointees and included scientists, Army Engineers, Naval Officers, and members of the U.S. Coast Survey. It was an efficient and effective organization. In 1910 Congress abolished the Lighthouse Board and created the Bureau of Lighthouses. The daily work of the

Lighthouse Service, however, continued without change.

Earlier, the lighthouses were far less organized and poorly operated. With the tremendous increase in waterborne commerce, greater efficiency was needed. Thus was born the Lighthouse Board.

It's hard for us today to fully realize the tremendous importance that shipping once held in America's daily life. There were no airplanes, semi-trailers or Federal Express and there were darn few trains. The majority of our commerce, both in terms of freight and passengers, moved on the water. Thus it was critical that those navigational aids be the best possible.

The new Board organized the lights into Districts, with each assigned an inspector. The Great Lakes was divided into the Tenth and Eleventh Districts. A later reorganization in 1886 resulted in the Tenth District consisting of Lakes Erie and Ontario; the Ninth District, Lake Michigan; and the Eleventh, Lakes Huron and Superior.

Since the Lighthouse Service was governed, as were nearly all government agencies of the time, by the "spoils system," there certainly were appointments to the lightkeeper's job based on politics rather than ability. And just as certain, there were problems with improperly kept lights.

The public outcry against the evils of the spoils system resulted in the passage by Congress in 1883 of the Pendleton Civil Service Act. Now appointments to key government positions would be based on ability and special examinations were required of applicants. Initially, only a very few agencies were covered by the Act. Later Presidents gradually increased the number. In 1896 President Grover Cleveland added the U.S. Lighthouses Service.

Construction

Generally speaking Great Lakes lighthouses were built during a relatively brief period of time and are very similar in construction. To withstand the ravages of Great Lakes storms, the lights were well built and extremely functional. They tended to be square and plain in design, with no emphasis placed on anything frivolous. The lights were not usually "one of a kind," but built from standard designs. For example, the nearby Au Sable Light, eight miles east of Grand Marais, and Outer Island Light in the Apostle Islands were both built in 1874 from the same plans. In many instances, however, the basic design was modified to meet a particular site requirement.

Usually the light would consist of a compound of several buildings; the light tower proper, Keeper's quarters, an oil house and a fog signal house. Depending on the design of the light, the tower could be incorporated as part of the Keeper's quarters. A pier or dock was also built to facilitate the landing of personnel and supplies.

Lamps, Lenses and Lights

The earliest lights on the Great Lakes used Argand lamps with parabolic reflectors. Complicated, they were inefficient and difficult to maintain, but were also the best available.

Between 1852-1859, nearly all the Great Lakes lights were given the new Fresnel lens. This lens has a powerful central lamp surrounded by refracting prisms and glass rings. The rings and prisms bend and guide the light, directing it outward in powerful beams. Invented in early 1820, the lens was named for Augustin Fresnel, a French scientist.

Fresnel lenses were classified into six sizes or orders, relating to their power. A sixth order lens was less than a foot in diameter, while a first order lens was six feet and stood nearly 12 feet high! The lenses were very expensive, but soon paid for themselves in reducing fuel costs, since they used only a quarter of previous requirements.

Up until roughly 1864, all of the Great Lakes lights, as well as all others, burned sperm whale oil. When its price increased to what the Lighthouse Service considered unacceptable levels, the fuel was changed, first to a lard oil and later to a mineral oil. In 1904 the ultimate improvement was made when the Service changed to the use of incandescent oil vapor. Today electric lamps provide the glow.

A third order Fresnel lens. Note the ring effect of the glass. Although expensive, the lenses were powerful beacons.

Fog Signals

Fog signals were usually maintained at all lights. At first they were only hand rung bells, but by 1851 mechanically rung bells were in use. Later steam whistles and sirens were tried. By 1900 nearly all fog signals were of the steam whistle variety. One problem with the steam whistle was the long time needed to start a fire to generate enough steam to sound the whistle. Often it took as long as 45 minutes. In a busy shipping channel, this was a very long time indeed. Eventually these signals were replaced with ones using compressed air. The air was provided by gasoline or diesel engines driving special air compressors.

Daily Routine

Daily routine at a lighthouse was difficult and demanding. It was also tedious and boring, depending on one's outlook. The light had to be maintained in a constant state of readiness. The lens had to be cleaned and polished, the lamp filled and wicks trimmed. It is from the wick trimming job that the old Keepers were often called "Wickies." Regulations called for the light to be ready for the evenings' use not later than 10 a.m. The grounds had to be kept clean and all buildings and facilities in good repair.

The exact details of the Keeper's responsibilities could be found in the publication *Instructions to Light-Keepers,* provided by the Lighthouse Board. Literally everything he needed to know was spelled out.

To help pass the time, and also provide fresh vegetables, Keepers often kept small gardens. Usually they were not very successful since the lights were located in inhospitable areas that did not have good soil. In some instances Keepers brought boxes of their own garden soil with them. This was for some years the practice of the Keeper at Stannard Rock Light. Located about 44 miles out in Lake Superior, nearly directly north from Marquette, the Light is often lashed by terrific storms. The Keeper continually "lost" his gardens. The tremendous waves just swept them away!

The Lighthouse Service also provided special "portable libraries," to help fight the boredom. Packed into boxes of 50 books each, they could be easily exchanged between stations. As an added bonus, the boxes were designed to stack into neat book shelves, thus helping to minimize the amount of furniture required.

The lonely lights were supplied by special vessels called lighthouse tenders. These tough vessels carried not only all the operating supplies needed by the lights, but also the dreaded Lighthouse Inspectors. These men were famous for their "white glove" examinations of the facility. A poor inspection could spell the end of a Keeper's career.

Some Keepers seemed to take the daily routine well. Others however, after a careful reading of their daily logs, appeared to "lose their marbles," at least to this writer's observation.

The Keepers

A lighthouse was often a family enterprise where the husband and wife teamed up to make the light successful. While the husband, as Keeper, was responsible for the maintenance of the light proper, the wife was held responsible for the upkeep of the quarters.

A favorite trick of the Lighthouse Inspectors, after carefully checking the husband's work was to privately pull the wife aside and mention to her that her husband wasn't keeping the light quite up to standard and perhaps she could encourage him more. When the inspector finished checking the quarters as maintained by the wife, he would privately tell her husband that his wife's work wasn't quite up to the required level. Could he encourage her more? We can only imagine the domestic tranquility that existed once the Inspector left!

Lightkeepers were no better paid than their Life-Saving counterparts. In 1867 salaries were fixed at $600 per year for Keepers and $420 for Assistant

Keepers. Although the Lighthouse Board considered the pay vastly inadequate, a parsimonious Congress did not increase the pay until 1917!

The Keepers kept journals, jotting down daily events. Such diaries are a fascinating glimpse into the past. The journals provide a comprehensive record of life at the lights, recording news of the Keeper's families, the arrival of the Lighthouse Inspectors, passage of lake vessels, daily chores, visitors and weather.

Originally the local Collectors of Customs nominated Keepers for their specific jobs. The Lighthouse Board either accepted or rejected the nominations. Final approval would be granted by the Secretary of the Treasury.

By the mid 1890s, an evaluation of the Keepers work was added, as was a special three-month probationary period for initial appointments. As the Lighthouse Service matured, Keepers often transferred between stations and Assistant Keepers regularly were promoted to Keepers as vacancies occurred.

The End

The Lighthouse Service ceased to exist in 1939 when it was absorbed into the Coast Guard. The days of the lonely Wickies were, like the days of the rip-roaring storm warriors of the Life-Saving Service, gone forever.

EARLY LIGHTS ON LAKE SUPERIOR

Major Lights, U.S. Waters

Copper Harbor 1849, rebuilt 1859
Whitefish Point 1849, rebuilt 1861
Manitou Island 1850, rebuilt 1861
Eagle Harbor 1850, refitted 1857
Ontonagon 1852, refitted 1857
Marquette 1853, refitted 1856
Point Iroquois 1855

Rock Harbor 1855
Round Island 1855, refitted 1864
Grand Island 1856
Portage River 1856
Michigan Island 1857
Minnesota Point 1857
Chequamegon Point 1858
Eagle River 1858
La Pointe 1858
Raspberry Island 1862
Gull Rock 1867
Huron Island 1868
Granite Island 1869
Mendota 1870
Au Sable Point 1874
Duluth Harbor 1874
Outer Island 1874
Portage Lake Ship Canal 1874
Menagerie Island 1875
Sand Island 1881
Passage Island 1882
Stannard Rock 1882
Grand Marais (Minnesota) 1885
Superior (pierhead) 1885
Devils Island 1891
Two Harbors 1892
Fourteen Mile Point 1894
Grand Marais (pierhead) 1895
Rock of Ages 1908
Split Rock 1910

The Dates For Some Lights Are Contradictory

Major Lights, Canadian Waters
Point Aux Pins 1873
Agate Island 1872
Michipicoten Island 1872
Porphyry Point 1873
Thunder Cape 1874

Battle Island 1877
Lamb Island 1877
Victoria Island 1881
Caribou Island 1886
Corbay Point 1889
Gargantua 1889
Peninsula Harbor 1891
Pie Island 1895

CRISP POINT LIGHT

Crisp Point Light was placed in operation in 1904. The 50-foot brick tower was located with the Crisp Point Life-Saving Station.

The light station was closed in 1930. In 1965 the various support buildings were razed by the Coast Guard. Today nothing is left except the tower, which erosion has placed precariously close to the water's edge.

Crisp Point Light (circa 1900). Today only the light tower is still standing.

Marquette Maritime Museum

An automatic battery powered beacon technically still keeps the light in operation. Its current nominal range is 12 miles.

Crisp Point Light today. Beach erosion has nearly toppled the tower.

POINT IROQUOIS LIGHT

The first light at Point Iroquois was erected in 1853 to help guide vessels entering and leaving the Soo Canal. The present brick tower was built in 1870 to replace the original wooden structure. Quarters for the Keeper were added at that time and quarters for the Assistant Keeper in 1902.

The light became obsolete in 1962 when a new automatic light was established at Gros Cap on the Canadian coast. In 1965 the light was taken out of service and transferred to the United States National Park Service.

The area is called Iroquois Point because it is the site where the Chippewa defeated the Iroquois in 1662.

Point Iroquois Light in 1975. Notice the way the Assistant Keepers qsuarters were added to the main structure.

Michigan State Archives

WHITEFISH POINT LIGHT

The historical records are not clear as to which light was the first on Lake Superior. Both Whitefish Point and Copper Harbor are given credit for 1849.

Because of its proximity to the Soo Canal, Whitefish Point Light is perhaps the most important on Lake Superior. Every vessel entering or leaving the lake must pass the Point. Historically, every upbound vessel uses Whitefish as its point of departure for setting

a course and downbound vessels make for Whitefish.
A reliable light was critical for safe navigation.

This 1906 photograph shows the ruins of the old stone
building that was built at the same time as the original
Whitefish Point light tower.

Michigan State Archives

The first light was a black, 65 foot high stone or
brick tower. The stone came from early Tahquamenon
Island. The base of the tower was 25 feet in diameter
with walls five feet thick. The top of the tower was
tapered to 12 feet. In the spring of 1849 the new light
was functioning. Also built at this time was a smalll
stone building. In 1861 the light was rebuilt. One
change was the color of the tower, from black to white.

The present 80-foot tower was built in 1902.
Next to the tower is a two-story frame lightkeepers
house. Also in the compound is a second two-story
house, a fog signal building, oil house and garage.

The original tower was fitted with thirteen Winslow
Lewis patent lamps with a 14 inch reflector. Sperm
whale oil was burned to provide the light. Later, when
the much more effective Fresnel lens became the norm,
one was fitted to the tower. Oil continued to be used

This panoramic view of Whitefish Point was taken from the top of the light tower. Notice how bare the area was of vegatation. The dotted line shows the location of the cable for an offshore submarine bell.

National Archives and Records Service

until 1913 when it was changed to an incandescent oil vapor lamp.

In April 1945 the light and Coast Guard Station were merged. At this time, the combined personnel numbered six men! In addition to manning the station, they also operated a weather station. The highest wind ever recorded at Whitefish Point by the Coast Guard was 96 miles per hour on August 26, 1966.

In 1970 the light was automated and the station closed. The present range of the light is 26 miles. In February, 1973, the station was placed on the National Register of Historic Sites.

Presently the facility is under lease to the Great Lakes Shipwreck Historical Society. It is intended to be developed as a shipwreck memorial museum dedicated to the men and vessels lost on the Great Lakes.

The 1,000-foot freighter STEWART J. CORT rounding Whitefish Point. The Point is still a major congestion point for Lake Superior commerce.

Author's Collection

Whitefish Point Light today. Since 1849 there has been a light on this dangerous point.

Author's Collection

ISLE PARISIENNE LIGHT

The Canadian lights also expanded to meet the needs of increased navigation. In 1868 there were 198 lights in the entire Dominion, most on the Great Lakes. By 1897, it had increased to 635.

The Isle Parisienne Light, located at the southwest tip of Parisienne Island' is still an active light and very important to Whitefish Bay navigation. The original light, consisting of a grey concrete hexagonal tower, double dwelling, fog alarm building, oil building, boat house and dock, was built during the period 1911-1912. It was fully operational in 1912.

REFERENCES:

Bogue, Margaret Beattie and Palmer, Virginia A.

271

AROUND THE SHORES OF LAKE SUPERIOR: A GUIDE TO HISTORIC SITES. University of Wisconsin Sea Grant College Program, 1979.

Correspondence, Public Archives of Canada, dated December 10, 1984 to Author.

Mansfield, J.B. *HISTORY OF THE GREAT LAKES.* (Chicago: J.H. Beers, 1899).

Noble, Dennis L. and O'Brien, Michael T. *SENTINELS OF THE ROCKS.* (Marquette, Michigan: Northern Michigan University Press, 1979).

O'Brien Michael T. *GUARDIANS OF THE EIGHTH SEA, A HISTORY OF THE COAST GUARD ON THE GREAT LAKES, 1976.*

Putnam, George R. *SENTINELS OF THE COAST, THE LOG OF A LIGHTHOUSE ENGINEER.* (New York: W.W. Norton, 1937).

Ripley, James M. "Whitefish Point Light". *INLAND SEAS, Winter 1968.*

Splake, T. Kilgore. *SUPERIOR LAND LIGHTS.* (Battle Creek, Michigan: Angst Productions, 1984).

GLOSSARY

Throughout the book I have frequently used terms and expressions that may be unfamiliar to the casual reader. I used them to keep the text as accurate as possible, as well as to provide a certain flavor of expression.

BEAM, BEAM ENDS. The greatest width of a vessel, she is on her beam ends when the beam is almost perpendicular to the water, generally caused by the cargo shifting.

CABLE. A heavy rope or chain, normally used attached to anchors or in towing.

DAVIT. Small cranes that project off the vessel's sides or stern for hoisting small boats. The yawl or lifeboat were kept on davits.

FORE BOOM. The spar of the fore mast to which the bottom of the sail is laced.

FORECASTLE. The forward compartment of a vessel, often the crews quarters.

GREAT LAKES SHIPWRECK HISTORICAL SOCIETY. Route 2, Box 279-A, Sault Ste. Marie, Michigan 49783; group organized to provide a memorial to the men and ships lost in the Great Lakes.

HEAD, VESSEL's HEAD, HEAD TO SEA. Keeping the bow into the sea and wind.

KEDGE ANCHOR. An anchor used for kedging or

warping, used to move a vessel by dropping an anchor and bringing the vessel up to it by hauling on the anchor cable.

KEWEENAW. Popular name for Michigan's Keweenaw Peninsula, landmark for sailors.

LIGHT. Without cargo, a vessel sailing in ballast is also often called light.

LYLE GUN. The life-saving gun used to fire a life line from shore to a vessel wrecked offshore, named for a Colonel Lyle of the U.S. Army Ordnance Corps, its inventor.

ORE. Iron ore from the Michigan or Minnesota mines, major Lake Superior iron ports were Two Harbors, Duluth, Superior, Ashland and Marquette.

PILOTHOUSE. Compartment where the steering wheel is located, usually located forward.

PORTAGE CANAL. Canal cutting the base of the Keweenaw Peninsula, used as a sheltered route to avoid heavy storms off the tip of the Keweenaw, copper shipping ports of Houghton, Hancock and Lake Linden were on the canal.

PROPELLERS. A new class of vessel called propeller because they used the new "Erickson screw propeller", provided greater capacity and economy, from 1840s-1860s revolutionized Great Lakes vessels.

PULL. To row, since a rowing crew faces to the stern, they pull at the oars.

SCHOONER-BARGE. New type of vessel that emerged on the Great Lakes as steam eclipsed sail, often modified schooners with topmasts removed along with sails and hamper except for fore, main and aft masts, groups of up to six could be towed behind steamers or special towing tugs, their sails could be used to help increase the speed of a tow if the wind was right, in heavy weather sails could also steady a tow, if towline broke they could still sail a rough course, very popular from 1870-1900s.

SOO. The popular expression for Sault Ste. Marie and the St. Mary's Falls Ship Canal.

SPONSON. Bulging part of a vessels hull, used to support machinery or add stability.

STEAM-BARGE. Early steamer designed for bulk cargos.

STRING. Term for a number of schooner-barges towed together.

WHIP. A single block with a line rove through it.

YAWL, YAWL BOAT. A heavy built square-sterned pulling work boat, usually 16-18 feet long, often carried at stern davits of schooners and small steamers, typically such vessels did not carry lifeboats.

Ask your bookstore salesperson for a complete listing of Avery Color Studios' Michigan and Great Lakes regional titles or send inquiries directly to Avery Color Studios, Star Route Box 275, Au Train, Michigan 49806.